EMPOWERING KINDNESS

NATHAN CALDWELL

ACKNOWLEDGMENTS

Special thanks to:

Bronwyn Botts, Todd Snapp, Thomas Earp, Jodi Costa,

Tom Goodlet, Sarah Williams, Holly Cole and Steven Crow

for your contribution in shaping this message

and getting it into the hands of others.

Extra special thanks to:

My wife Holly for being a tremendous listener,

advice giver and going along with me on this crazy adventure.

My kids Grayson, Teagan, and Rex.

There's no motivation greater in my life than caring for my kids.

This book is dedicated to my father, Rob Caldwell,
For being my inspiration to understand kindness
and my motivation to pass it on to others.

I've got a lot to learn and a long way to go
but I keep hoping I'll be just like him when I grow up.

TABLE OF CONTENTS

FOREWORD

I met Nathan Caldwell when I was the keynote speaker for a major software conference in 2015. He was the show director and responsible for making me look and sound good on stage. He was also responsible for all of the video messaging shared from the stage including a powerful video to introduce my speech, which was a surprise to me. You know how there are some people who, when you meet them, you feel like you want to know them better? That is Nathan. He was (and no doubt still is) a consummate professional. He also has a compelling enthusiasm and warmth that draws you to him.

It came as no surprise to me that Nathan was writing a book... any book. He is a deep thinker. Nor did it surprise me to learn that his book was about kindness. As Nathan and I worked together during the conference and following it, I found in him a man with an abiding sense of charity toward others (including me), a radiant positive demeanor, and a desire to make everyone's world a little better. In other words, Nathan manifests kindness. He walks the walk.

In *Empowering Kindness*, Nathan uses the power of personal stories, pop culture examples, and hard research to make the case for kindness. From his list of *4 Keys to Kindness* to stories about celebrities including Dolly Parton and Wayne Gretzky, and personal anecdotes, he delivers persuasive examples of the power of kindness at work in building human-to-human bridges. He makes the case for kindness as a tool for preventing heart disease and improving workplace productivity through the powerful mood-altering effects of kindness.

As you read *Empowering Kindness*, you become clearly aware of the role of kindness in building and enhancing relationships at work, with your partner, and among friends. You also gain insights into the power of kindness as a tool for personal growth.

Whether you're concerned about some of the toxicity in modern culture, our seeming inability to civilly disagree with each other, shaming culture, or any of the other dark clouds that seem endemic in contemporary life, *Empowering Kindness* provides a look into a world of light, compassion, and empathy. Accompanying that view are practical techniques you and your colleagues, friends, and family can put to work immediately to help soothe old hurts and pave new pathways to relationships founded on kindness, caring, and mutual respect.

As I finished reading *Empowering Kindness*, I was left with a sense of hope for the future, a belief that making kindness-based behavior choices is not just a viable path, but an absolutely necessary path for all humankind.

Give yourself a gift of hope, optimization, and a renewed faith in humanity. Read this book, take its lessons to heart, and spread the power of kindness!

Don R. Crawley
Author of *The Compassionate Geek*
@doncrawley

INTRODUCTION

Big changes were happening in my life. Changes in my career. Baby #3 on the way. A storm of uncertainty closing in around me. As I put my toddlers to bed and lay beside them night after night, the gears in my head kept turning. I asked myself what am I meant to do?

As a child, I read comic books and knew every hero's origin story inside and out. Spider-Man was bitten by a radioactive spider. The Incredible Hulk was blasted with gamma radiation. Now, I never hoped for some tragic event to happen just so I could realize what I was meant to do but I somehow had the fantasy that at some point it would just hit me. It seemed to happen to real people all the time. Wayne Gretzky was skating by 2.5 years old, Dolly Parton sang on the Grand 'Ol Opry when she was just 13. It amazed me to even have friends who knew from a young age what they wanted to do, went to school for it and then became it.

I searched my head and my heart and one night, while lying beside my kids, I started thinking about my dad.

My dad was a letter carrier. He knew everyone on his route and would stop and speak to them any time he would run into them around town. A simple trip to the local grocery store would always turn into a multi-hour errand because he would stop and talk to everyone in the store since he at some point had delivered mail to them. It was part of who he was to know when someone on his route could use a helping hand. Many days after work, he would come home, change into paint-splattered jeans and an old worn-out t-shirt, grab a pair of work gloves, his toolbox and me, and we'd head to someone's house who he only knew from delivering mail. One of those ladies had experienced the loss of a brother. She had no one to assist her in clearing out her brother's house and garage. So, day after day, my dad took me along to take loads of hoarded items to the dump or to her church for a rummage sale. We weren't being paid; we were helping because someone was in need. My dad taught me what kindness looks like as part of a person's character. That being kind is the first instinct, the expectation of the person executing it, i.e., the attitude of "Of course I'm going to help, it's what I do."

We didn't have much money growing up, but we could give of our time and care about people. That lady became Auntie Ann to our whole family and has been a regular at our family Thanksgivings, birthdays, and weddings.

My dad was my example of empowering kindness.

He was kind, taught me to be kind, and gave me the ability to be kind. Because he has lived his whole life this way, I also have the benefit of seeing the positive outcomes of a life dedicated to being kind. I don't know of a happier more joyful person or more respected and appreciated man than my dad. That alone is enough for me to know I want to be kind.

I've taken the principle of kindness with me into the business world. I've experienced and seen the outcomes of leaders who are kind and those who aren't. I've seen kind leaders have more people on their teams who enjoy coming to work and consistently achieve exceptional performance. I've seen kind leaders experience less turnover and grow more members of their team into leadership roles.

I've also seen people accomplish amazing things that go above and beyond what we thought was ever possible all because they were inspired by kindness.

I began thinking about kindness a little differently. I began wondering if it is an actual superpower we each possess? It can accomplish so many positive outcomes, yet there are still leaders who do not embrace it.

While thinking about my dad, thinking about kindness and what I had observed about positive leadership, I developed this theory:

A business that leads with kindness will be more successful, have more joyful employees and inspire others to do amazing things.

In this book, I've collected scientific research and inspiring stories that demonstrate the impact kindness can have on your business.

My hope is to have you join me on the mission of being kind and providing your people with the understanding and capabilities to also be kind.

This is my origin story, what will be yours?

CHAPTER ONE

A COMPLETELY APPROPRIATE DOUBLE ENTENDRE

I imagine a world where we can be joyful humans who help each other, build each other up, and achieve greater success because we do good for each other.

The message of this book doesn't stop with you saying, "Oh, I get it: it's like paying it forward or random acts of kindness. Someone ahead of you pays for your coffee in the drive-through, so you, in turn, pay for the coffee of someone behind you." While those types of efforts are great and good and fun and produce benefits, I want to add a few layers that will help you create a culture of kindness within your organization.

Empowering Kindness is a title that has two truths hidden in plain sight.

1. It's a descriptive verb. An action. A mission. Empower those in your circle of influence, your people, to be kind by being kind to

your people, giving them the opportunity and ability to be kind to others, and equip them to teach others to be kind.

2. When you are kind, it is empowering. The outpouring of kindness to others makes you feel good. (Feel good is oversimplified; check out the science of it all in Chapter 3, where we'll cover several studies on the physical, psychological, and organizational health benefits of engaging in kindness.)

Is there a need?

Kindness isn't just a nice-to-have. There's an actual need, especially when considering the effect that a lack of kindness in your company culture can have on your customers. It's a staggering statistic that 79% percent of companies don't empower their employees to provide great customer experiences. This is a contributing factor to the confusion and disconnect that companies are believing about themselves, i.e., 80% of CEOs think their company delivers great customer experiences, but only 8% of customers share that their experience was great. [1]

The term customer service is misleading when policies supersede service. In 2008, a musician named Dave Carroll was flying United Airlines when his Taylor guitar was broken while in United's possession. He went through nine months of run around trying to find someone at United that would actually care. Instead, the final word from United was that they would do nothing about it and would not return any more of his calls or emails. At that point, Dave decided to share his experience in song form

1. https://www.maritzcx.com/blog/general/customer-employee-recognition-engagement/;
   https://www.bain.com/insights/closing-the-delivery-gap-newsletter/

and created three music videos singing all about United breaking his guitar and the unsympathetic response he received. The music videos that Dave shared on YouTube ended up going viral and attracting stories by the L.A. Times, CNN, and calls from The Late Show with David Letterman and Bob Taylor, the owner of Taylor Guitars. The videos have generated over 22 million views. It is a powerful example of a company upholding their policies rather than giving their people the ability to show kindness to a customer. On the opposite side of the spectrum, Bob Taylor, reached out to Dave and gave him two new Taylor guitars and issued a video offering his support of Dave and any other musicians who had unfortunately experienced damage to their guitars.

As a leader, you have direct control to create a great customer experience by increasing your company's ability to be kind. Creating a culture of kindness and providing your people with the resources they need to be kind will affect the way your company works together internally as well as how your company treats any external customers or contacts. If United Airlines were focused on empowering kindness, their customer service agents would have had the freedom to find a solution to the broken guitar and Dave's frustrations wouldn't have mounted for nine months. Instead, they suffered the consequences of a customer service publicity nightmare. It got so bad for United Airlines that four days after Dave's song appeared on YouTube, United's stock dropped by 10 percent [2], a $180 million loss. Talk about a case of turbulence!

---

2. https://web.archive.org/web/20100531204013/http://www.timesonline.co.uk/tol/comment/columnists/chris_ayres/article6722407.ece

A lack of kindness within your organization will lead to a lack of kindness being out-poured from your organization.

Kindness is needed and it isn't enough to tell people to be nicer. It must become your culture and it begins with you leading by example.

You set the tone for kindness when you demonstrate compassion, empathy, elevated service, and good deeds with pure motives.

Mike Fisher played in the NHL for 18 seasons before retiring in 2018. He was drafted by the Ottawa Senators in 2000. He played for them until February 2011, when the Senators General Manager, Bryan Murray stopped by the locker room and asked Mike to see him. Mike didn't know what was about to happen. Bryan spoke simply and said, "Well, Fish, I've traded ya."

Mike was completely shocked and crushed until Bryan followed up with these words:

"I've got some good news for you, though. You're going to Nashville."

Mike shared his reaction in an article in The Player's Tribune. [3]

"Oh my goodness. Talk about some life-changing words. I could have been going to 28 other cities, but I was actually going to Nashville, where I could finally be with my wife full-time."

If you aren't familiar, Mike Fisher married Carrie Underwood, the country music superstar, only 7 months prior. They were newlyweds and it wasn't easy being split between Ottawa and Nashville.

The Senators' owner, Eugene Melnyk called Mike and told him the

3. https://www.theplayerstribune.com/en-us/articles/mike-fisher-nashville-predators-one-way-ticket

reason for the trade, "You know Fish, I just wanted you to be with your wife."

Mike described what Eugene and Bryan had done for him.

"When trade talks had heated up, a few teams had been interested in me, but Eugene and Bryan agreed to make sure that my destination would be Nashville. They could have traded me anywhere, but they were genuinely looking out for me and my family. That's what makes hockey such a special sport, even at the NHL level. Yes, it's a business, but the amount of good human beings I've run across in this sport is just incredible.

I know God was looking out for me that day, and sometimes he uses good people like Eugene and Bryan to carry out his plans. So I'll just take the time now to thank all three of them for the one-way ticket."

These two businessmen showed kindness and pure motives by forgoing any other advantageous deals that may have been on the table. They acted in the best interest of an individual that had dedicated 11 years to their organization. As a result, it put a family together in the same city and caused Mike to have such incredible gratitude.

Having pure motives to act with others best interests in mind leads to incredibly powerful examples of genuine kindness.

An enemy of genuine kindness is to engage in kindness with the motive to undermine others. Doing nice things for others with twisted motives corrupts the entire system. If you are kind to others just to get something in return or to make yourself look good in front of others, you will miss the benefits of being kind.

How do you make sure your kindness is coming from the proper place? You must be self-reflective, self-aware, and remove ulterior motives, so that kindness has room to grow within your character. Here are four key areas to spend some time reflecting on your motivation and mindset towards kindness.

KEYS TO KINDNESS

1. How you feel about kindness

What are your feelings about being kind? Do you believe in being kind?

If you do not believe in kindness, you won't be able to convince others to believe in it.

Are you implementing plans/perks/values that you and your people truly care about or are you just going through the motions? Are you begrudgingly adding plans/perks/values to your company because other companies are doing it or do you truly believe in them?

A company that thinks they need volunteer events because other companies their size do it misses out on the benefits and effectiveness of actually being passionate about a cause or organization and devoting themselves to it. A department that refers to itself as a team but commonly uses the phrase "that's not my job" misses out on the growth that comes with relying on each other, passing the ball, receiving the ball, and working together for the big win.

Have you ever heard someone in an organization use the term "family" when they haven't earned it? There's an episode of The Office, where the manager, Michael Scott asks his people to do a comedy roast of him. One of the warehouse workers, Daryl, says to Michael, "You say we're a family here. What's that guy's name?" as he points to another warehouse worker. Michael Scott takes a couple of guesses before he's told that he gave him a ride home last week. Michael guesses wrong again, then he is told that the warehouse worker's name is also Michael. The term "family" should not be used flippantly. It will come off as insincere and out of touch if you are not living up to it. Some may even have a distaste toward the term "family" because it may draw out negative feelings or experiences. It's okay to allow family to be family and work to be work. If you do insist on calling your environment "family," be extra careful about your hiring process, because, once they're on board, it looks highly suspicious to say, "You're family" and then have to let someone go. I couldn't imagine sitting my kids down and telling one of them, "I feel like you're just not a good fit anymore, so we're letting you go." Those decisions must be made at times in a business, but it does make the term "family" problematic. Am I saying that kindness means that you can never let someone go? No, not at all. But, part of being self-reflective is determining if you believe in giving your people the opportunity to perform well.

Your leadership position means you are responsible to elevate people and align them with the direction of the company.

All of your company values need to come from a place of sincere kindness. You must truly feel it and believe in it, not just think it's what people want to hear.

2. How you act

Are you following through with being kind?

This is the "Walk the Talk" portion.

Occasionally, people will act a certain way that seems in opposition to the stance they take. If questioned, they often use the phrase, "You don't know me." as a defense of their motives. Actions communicate what you truly believe about a topic. You could give off a message that betrays what you say your company's core values are. If you say your company has unlimited PTO, but each time an employee books time off he/she receives a guilt trip from the manager, the only conclusion is a "yeah but." "Yeah, they offer unlimited PTO, but they don't really want you to ever use it." Especially if that is passed on in any of the subtext surrounding the plan. Managers will often ask, "What if my employees start to abuse it?" If the response is, "Don't worry, Mr. Manager, statistically speaking employees with unlimited PTO tend to take less time off than those that have a bank of days. When people have a bank of days, they take their maximum amount of days because if they don't use it, they'll lose it. Also, they still have to get approval from you. We believe this will be an attractor for recruiting and will help us in competing in the job market." What does this communicate to everyone in the company? That it will be unlimited PTO in name only and that you can be as restrictive as you please. So, instead of becoming a company that has employees who are refreshed, connected with their families, and inspired, you have a company that just puts a new benefit on their "what we offer" page with an invisible asterisk.

I spotted an article where the company, *SteelHouse*, gives unlimited PTO and a $2,000 spending budget for each employee to take the time off. What does it do for employees? It recharges them and builds enthusiasm. They feel valued and believe that the company actually means it when they say unlimited PTO is a benefit.

The same is true with any other value a company introduces. Dave Ramsey's organization believes in community service and gives its employees five days PTO to be used for volunteering on top of its PTO plans. What does this show? By its actions, it is saying that they care about volunteering.

You must reflect on whether or not you are following through with what you say and being kind.

3. How you value others

Do you put others above yourself? Why is this a separate pillar? Because you could feel that you want to be kind to others, you could even go through with the actions, but there needs to be some self-reflection on your part about how much you value others.

A study was done that compared people who did not participate in philanthropic activities, those who did for personal benefit, and those who did for altruistic reasons. After 20 years, out of those who did not participate at all, 4.3% had passed away. Of those who were philanthropic but for their own personal benefit, 4% had passed away. But for those who participated in philanthropic activities for altruistic reasons, only 1.6% had passed away. [4]

The truth is that we cannot trick the system. We cannot be kind just because we want the benefits. Our brains are hardwired to benefit us when we perform kindness altruistically. Part of sincere kindness is caring about

4. https://www.apa.org/pubs/journals/releases/hea-31-1-87.pd

the people we are being kind to. A leader who values their people will make decisions with their people's best interests in mind.

4. How you use your resources

Do you have power over your resources to help?

Even if you feel that you believe in kindness, act in kindness and value others but do not take control of your resources and use them for kindness, you will not be effective.

As a leader, you are deciding every day how your people will use company money, company time and company talent. Are you prioritizing these resources to emphasize kindness?

You may have heard people say that if something is truly important to you, then you will prioritize and make it happen. But what if you haven't learned yet what should be important to you? What if you have been conditioned to believe in chasing things that do not ultimately matter as much as being kind?

In order to truly be kind, some self-reflection concerning your resources needs to happen. You've probably heard the expression that your last words will never be, "I only wish I'd spent more time at work" or "The most important lesson I learned from my career was to not care about anyone else and just get ahead."

When put that way, it's easy to see the truth and humor because you think to yourself "Yup, I spend way too much time at work." And you do! Do the math: working 8 a.m. to 5 p.m., Monday through Friday, plus commute averages 11.5 hrs/day committed to working at a minimum!

There have been many days when I left for work in the morning while our baby was sleeping and got home after he was back in bed and thought, "Wow! I have to wait until the weekend to spend time with him."

With that much time devoted to work and also wanting to spend time with my family, it's easy to rationalize there's no way I could also squeeze in giving time to others who may need help. I've also seen others feel the strain financially or feeling they have nothing to contribute when people with much higher salaries come asking for contributions to a cause.

Sometimes, your employees are held back from using their resources to do kind things for others due to the tight constraints brought on by their work environment. I've seen employees with zero flexibility in their schedule, pay scale, and autonomy change from a helpful and kind person to one who exhibits stress, panic, and drama in almost all situations. A simple, "Hey, I was wondering..." gets answered with, "I don't have time for this." Or resentment builds toward the company when some teams are given flexibility in their schedule to run personal errands or work from home, and others are not afforded that same freedom.

Dedicating the resources of company money, time, and talent towards kindness gives your people the opportunity to experience kindness and the freedom to be kind to others they may not have been afforded before.

Think about the positive outcomes of giving your people an annual stipend for charitable donations or the opportunity to nominate a cause or charity they are passionate about. Or the positive outcomes of giving your people guilt-free time in their schedule to assist a team other than their own. Or creating a partnership with a deserving organization in the community, putting your talents to use and making an ongoing impact.

These Keys to Kindness will help you reflect on your sincerity and motivation. You must begin from a sincere place and from there teach your people what kindness is, and your expectations for executing kindness within your organization.

The concept of *Empowering Kindness* can be summed up in a few efforts:

- Be kind to your people.
- Give them the opportunity and ability to be kind to others.
- Equip them to teach others to be kind.

Beginning with you and your leadership team, you must lead by example giving your people the opportunity to experience and learn from these 7 benefits of Empowering Kindness:

1. First-hand knowledge of what it feels like to have something kind done for them

You cannot assume your people have experienced an act of kindness. You also have an opportunity to teach them what you define as kindness. Some of your people may have a skewed understanding of kindness. It is important to demonstrate what you define as kindness. There are benefits to experiencing kindness from a leader. It communicates directly to your people that you care about them and you like them which speaks volumes to the inner psyche of your employees. Showing kindness to an employee gives them a feeling of belonging and acceptance.

Once they know what it feels like to have something kind done for them, they become curious about others feeling the same way if they are kind to them. It also serves as your example for the expectation and execution of kind behavior.

2. First-hand knowledge of how to recognize the opportunity to do something kind for someone else

A key element in being kind is training to see the need and opportunity for kindness. It's easy for you to know what you need personally. You know when you're tired and when you're hungry. But it's not so easy to recognize when there's a need or opportunity to be kind to an employee. It requires effort to be aware of how another person is feeling. This takes time. You have to speak to people and get to know their personalities so you can recognize when they are experiencing an off day. Is that person tired, hungry, stressed, confused, okay, or not okay? Being aware of the status of the individuals around you increases your skills at recognizing when and how you should be kind to others. My best recommendation is to not wait until something is wrong with your employee to do something kind for them. Do kind things regularly. It is amazing how often people will seem okay, then you do something nice for them and then they open up and share that they have been having a horrible week.

3. First-hand knowledge of what it feels like to do something kind for someone else

Not all of your people are experienced at doing kind things for others. It is important to give your people this experience because doing something kind for someone feels very different than having something kind done for you. When your employees do something kind for another individual it allows them to understand deeper feelings of compassion, grace, mercy, and forgiveness.

4. Autonomy, authority, and resources to do something kind for someone else

Commission your people to create solutions that are kind and give them the support they need to accomplish this. A majority of employees experience greater job satisfaction when they have the freedom to create or at least contribute to the solution of a problem they are facing.

This may look different depending on the size of your company or the field that you're in. A budget for a 25 person company is going to be drastically different than a 10,000 person company. You may have to create some parameters based on your size, industry, and make-up, but the fact remains that job satisfaction increases when employees can participate and contribute to solutions.

5. Mental, physical, and organizational health benefits are achieved by everyone in the experience

For the leader: the one who is empowering the employee to do kind actions.

For the employee: the one who performs the kind actions.

For the customer: the one who receives the kind actions.

For the organization: the one whose culture is changed by the kind actions.

Everyone benefits from being involved in kindness. Kindness produces endorphins that combat heart disease, stress, depression, increase joy, and even extends life. [5]

Chapter 3 covers this in more detail, but for now, it's important to realize that physical and mental health benefits are achieved by everyone involved in the act of kindness.

6. Inspiration to those who witness the kind actions

Kindness has such powerful positive effects that even just seeing someone be kind can be an inspiration to do great things. It is especially inspirational to see someone you have invested in and coached rise through the ranks and experience success.

7. Team and organizational growth

Empowering kindness expands the leadership skills of those who are coaching others and provides room for those who are being coached, to be kind. It gives those who are learning kindness pride in what they do. It increases job satisfaction, loyalty, and leadership growth.

It gives those who are learning the honor of understanding the benefits of being kind to others. It creates true teamwork, where people rely on each other, contribute to each other's success, bring out the best in each other, celebrate each other's accomplishments, and ultimately celebrate the team wins.

What if you lead your company to embrace kindness as the leading factor in your company's culture? What if you did it shoulder to shoulder

5. https://www.huffpost.com/entry/can-kindness-cut-the-risk_b_799562 David R. Hamilton Ph.D.

with fellow leaders and employees?

How many people would then begin to understand the culture? How many would begin to understand that they work with people who truly care about others?

You can't just say you care, you've got to show you care, invite others to join, and, in so doing, you will teach them what it is like to be kind. It will shape your character to the point where you can't help but be kind. Demonstrating compassion, empathy, elevated service, and good deeds will become second nature and bring with it all the benefits of being kind.

With so many benefits, it's hard to imagine why so many people wouldn't already believe in creating a culture of kindness.

Perhaps it's because of a few lies you've probably heard.

CHAPTER TWO
THE LIES WE BELIEVE: KINDNESS KILLERS

Why can't we be kind to one another?

Is kindness in opposition to accomplishing your personal goals of growth and advancement?

Why do so many people believe the proper way to operate in life is to look out for themselves and not each other?

Why are bullying, depression, and suicide so prevalent?

Why are so many people unhappy in their careers?

Why is meanness often being promoted?

Perhaps these questions are answered by a few lies many people have believed.

"Nice guys finish last."

"Look out for number one."

"You can't make an omelet without breaking a few eggs."

"You have to step on people to get ahead."

"It's not personal; it's business."

"Winning isn't everything. It's the only thing."

These statements are often just accepted. Why? Think about them. Do you really believe in them?

Let's start with "Nice guys finish last." The standard impression or meaning behind this phrase is you have to be mean or play dirty to get what you want and get ahead.

Does anyone really believe that nice people are the losers? What person on his/her death bed ever says, "I just wish I was more of a jerk in life, so I wouldn't have finished last." The real truth is nice guys never finish last. Nice people are the ones with healthy relationships, who have joy in helping others, and experience many more benefits that this book will explore. But for now, let's look deeper into these lies.

"Look out for number one."

If you only look out for number one, when you finally get to the top, you'll find it quite lonely.

"You can't make an omelet without breaking a few eggs."

This phrase typically means that, on your way to creating something that you view as a great goal, there will be some casualties. You can't accomplish anything of significance without others suffering some type of consequence.

But think about what really happens when making an omelet. When you break open an egg, you are actually unlocking its potential, bringing it into the mix to create a breakfast masterpiece. You are pushing that egg beyond its comfort zone and into what could possibly be its greatest achievement—brunch! Have you ever been in the presence of an omelet station? It is an incredible morning miracle. Boom! This phrase just got spun on its head, and now it means something completely new. Creating a great omelet isn't found in the breaking of eggs, it is found in bringing the eggs together and building something better together. Instead of thinking we will have to endure casualties along the way to create something great, we can look at it as bringing everyone together to create something great.

"You have to step on people to get ahead."

Ah, now I get to reference Dolly Parton, my heart coach. In her song *9 To 5*, this concept is from the perspective of the people who are getting stepped on. The line is "You're just another step on the boss man's ladder." The boss man is following through with each of the lies in this chapter. He is growing his stature, reputation, and wealth at the expense of his employees. He doesn't build anyone up other than himself. He manages his people through fear. He destroys trust and weakens the potential of each of the people he steps on.

Think of how many problems you could avoid in your company if everyone who applied for a supervisor or leadership position had to share their honest motivations during job interviews.

"Hello, thank you for interviewing me. Just so you know, I won't appreciate any of the employees you put on my team. I'll keep them around as long as they make me look good, and, if they're ever late or annoy me, I'll be done with them."

It would make the interview process that much easier.

True leadership is helping others climb over challenges instead of stepping over people. There is currently a leadership deficit in the workforce so you must not only be looking for great leadership talent but also cultivating leaders. Identify your people who have a talent for helping others and invest in them. Don't promote people who are the most technically proficient but have not shown any inclination toward empowering others to be kind. You will end up with employees who have the responsibility to take care of others but don't know how.

A leader's most important skill is kindness, not technical expertise. Dolly herself states that she's not the most technically proficient singer or songwriter, but by God, she has empowered countless people with her kindness.

Dollywood, Imagination Library, graduates from her high school, anyone who has listened to her song "Smoky Mountain Memories," even the self-freeing quotation to chase your dreams, "Find out who you are and do it on purpose." Good golly Miss Dolly, I thank you! Each of her business ventures is fully thought-out, as her momma would say, "to bring a blessing" or as I would say, "to empower kindness." Take Dollywood, for example, the theme park in Pigeon Forge, Tennessee, just outside the town where she grew up. Not only has she provided many forms of employment for people in the area, but she has programs set up to ensure her employees are shown kindness. Dollywood has health programs in-house, leadership programs, and an on-site chaplain who focuses on being connected with employees for prayer and faith-based counsel. She also demonstrates kindness with everyone she interacts with. I've spoken personally with employees of every level at the park, and her kindness is legendary. I recall speaking to an employee who was collecting parking fees in the toll booth. She shared a story with me about Dolly stopping by the booth and asking about how she and her family were doing. They were so deep in conversation that Dolly's assistants had to usher her along to her scheduled appointments. Dolly gave her time, but is that the great takeaway? Or is the great takeaway that Dolly is nice enough to speak to an employee regardless of role? Almost. Dolly doesn't just think it's important for her to be kind to someone who works within her organization. She thinks it's important to demonstrate kindness to everyone. She sees every employee as an extension of her own brand of kindness. The tollbooth employee now understands the expectation of how to treat customers and fellow employees because the leader of her company showed it to her. The message was clearly shared and passed on.

Dolly's kindness goes beyond her park and into people's homes. Have you heard of Dolly's Imagination Library? She has created a nonprofit (beginning first in her hometown but has since spread) that gives kids one book a month from the time they're born until they enter kindergarten. The first book she sends these babies is *The Little Engine That Could*. The message of believing in yourself is an inspiration to Dolly, and she wants to share that message with as many people as possible. When I say "as many as possible," I mean that she has given over 125 million books to children around the world. It has literally become the largest literacy program in the world.

In another effort to empower kindness in her hometown, in 2016 when the fires spread through the Smoky Mountains, Dolly opened up her heart and provided $1,000/month for six months to over 900 families who lost their homes in the fire. She also provided a $4500 scholarship to every middle and high school student whose family was affected by the fires. What did this do for those people? It got a whole county back on their feet. Sure, the money was helpful, but what will last beyond the money is the message of kindness, which was described over and over as a hand-up, not a handout. The difference is all in the attitude of the recipient. The recipients of the My People Fund and those witnessing it benefited from more than the dollar value. It serves as a catalyst for those who experience the kind act to pass that kindness on to others.

In the moment of adversity, when shown kindness, it becomes a personal and emotional understanding of how to treat others. This visceral experience is not easily forgotten and is subconsciously recalled at any moment you are given the opportunity to be kind to another person.

Circling back to the line Dolly shares in *9 To 5* "You're just another step on the boss man's ladder." Dolly gains much of her inspiration from real-life experiences. There was a time in her life when it was eerily similar to being held down just like a rung on that ladder. She had joined Porter Wagoner, a successful male country performer, on his tour and as a co-star on his television show. Soon her success began to overshadow him. She wanted to move on and grow her career but he became angry and bitter toward her. She even wrote *I Will Always Love You* to show her appreciation for what he had done for her. I share all this to emphasize that you must not allow good talented people who have kindness in their hearts to be unjustly held back in your organization. You must recognize those people and give them opportunities to do great things. There is no doubt that if you give your kind people opportunities, training and support to succeed that they will create the most beautiful and powerful solutions.

"It's not personal; it's business."

HUMAN RESOURCES sounds cold and unempathetic. The thought that humans are just used as resources, that everything they have is being depleted, and, as soon as the resources of that human are burned up from stress, overworking, underappreciation, or coldness, you can just toss them out because they aren't performing as they used to. Or you detach the accomplishments from the individual.

There's a line in *Erin Brockovich* where Ed Masry, played by Albert Finney, says "You make this personal, and it isn't." Erin Brockovich, played by Julia Roberts, responds with, "Not personal? That is my work! My sweat! My time away from my kids! If that's not personal, I don't know what is."

You must recognize that you are entering into a personal relationship with the people you employ. It doesn't get any more personal than spending the majority of your time together and engaging in a daily dependence upon each other. You laugh together, experience stress, deadlines, and victories together. You cheer each other on through milestones, and even show each other pictures of your kids or your dogs. A person's career is personal. They have been devoting themselves to this effort and spending years in this pursuit. It must not be treated casually.

"Winning is everything."

A study conducted by the US Army discovered that the higher someone climbs in collegiate sports, the more their moral fiber is deteriorated. The study showed that the higher the competition, the fewer players would display moral character. Winning cannot be everything. We can't ask people to sacrifice what makes them special and unique, the very things they have resolve in, just to have a quick win for the company. What is that worth? Does the commission of a sale equal the value of sacrificing what makes them who they are? You must stand up and protect the moral character that interested you in them as an employee when they were hired. If you erode the morals of your employees, you will erode the morals of your company.

As we pursue more lofty goals and pressure mounts it's easy to rationalize and fall for some of these lies. If you find yourself falling for some of these lies, perhaps it is because you have a short-sighted vision of what your goals should be.

It's important to evaluate your motivation when creating your goals in order to maintain a positive direction.

Your goals as a leader should never cause you to lose sight of making your people better. Your legacy is what you build in other people's lives.

The beautiful thing is that you will be even more successful when you're kind.

It feels better at the top when you aren't lonely.

Wayne Gretzky

I'm a Canadian who was a kid through the '80s–'90s. I collected hockey cards and watched The Great One play.

The amazing thing about The Great One wasn't just that he scored a lot of goals, it was that he was great for the sport of hockey. His attitude on and off the ice centered around never doing anything that would hurt the sport of hockey.

In hockey, games are won or lost by goals, but part of a player's statistics are tracked in points. A point is given for each goal a player scores and for each assist a player makes.

Wayne Gretzky was such an amazing player that he earned more points than any other player in history. He earned so many points that if you took away all of his goals, he'd still have more points from his assists than the combined goals and assists of any other players in the history of the game.

All-Time Points Leader
Wayne Gretzky, total points: 2,857
Goals/points from goals: 894
Assists/points from assists: 1,963
2nd Place:
Jaromir Jagr, total points: 1,921

He was focused on helping his teammates perform well, giving them opportunities to shoot and score. Even down to his selection of sticks. Gretzky famously played with a stick that had almost zero curve for the purpose of passing. While reducing the curve of his stick resulted in less speed in his shot, it increased his accuracy in passing from the front and back of his stick. He wanted to set up his teammates for glory.

The greatest hockey player ever, and he was focused on his teammates.

Was he competitive? Of course! Did he have the drive? Absolutely! Did he want his team to beat other teams? Definitely! He was excited about the win, but he didn't let ego or selfishness destroy his caring for the game. And he recognized the game is made up of players.

Do you have that same attitude related to your endeavors? So much respect for life and recognizing that life is made up of other people and their contributions, actions, and needs that you do all you can to honor the game? That you make choices to set others up for success? That even if all of your personal accomplishments dissolved into thin air, the sum of what you did for others outweighs what you accomplished for yourself? What if, because of the kindness you empowered others with, you were known as their Great One?

It makes you want to pass the puck more, doesn't it?

The example of Gretzky shows that there is a great opportunity for success while still being kind. Along this path of empowering others, there is an opportunity for personal growth, goals, and achievements. Plus, when you accomplish your goals, you have others there with you to celebrate.

There is no limit to the power that kindness can have. More powerful than any opposition or deterrent.

When you are empowering someone to be kind, you don't know how much power you've just equipped that person with. It could be that he or she goes on to empower one other person to be kind or thousands.

Seeing the results of what you've done for someone in their lives may take time because people don't often understand the value at the moment or have the wisdom to thank you right away. It can take time for the seeds of understanding and perspective to germinate and compel them to go back to the one who unlocked it in them. Even if you don't hear from them it could still be at work within them. It can become a part of their conscience's narrative, their internal personal trainer. The Mick to their Rocky.

If someone has empowered you to be kind and you have an internal recording of their voice cheering you on, it's important to share with them what a difference they have made in keeping you from falling prey to the lies we've believed.

CHAPTER THREE

SELF-LESS IS MORE: OUR BRAINS ARE HARDWIRED TO BENEFIT FROM BEING KIND

For a few pages, I'll share some studies that closely link being kind to our mental, physical and organizational health. You have a lot to gain if you are kind to your people and the positive results are multiplied exponentially when you build kindness into your culture and give all of your people the ability to be kind. Through these studies, you'll begin to see why kindness needs to be a distinct leader in creating your company culture.

KINDNESS, THE SILENT LIFE-GIVER.

Let's talk about heart disease, the number-one killer in the United States, claiming 635,260 lives annually. [1]

---

1. https://www.healthline.com/health/leading-causes-of-death

We know that proper diet, exercise, and maintaining a healthy weight are combatants against this number-one killer. But what you may not realize is that being kind to others also helps combat heart disease. Being kind to others produces oxytocin in your brain and heart, making its way through your cardiovascular system resulting in many positive health benefits. Oxytocin is known to cause an incredible decrease in free radicals and inflammation. A decrease in inflammation means a decrease of plaque in your arteries and, as a result, a much lower risk for heart disease and, specifically, a heart attack. [2]

The same medical marvel, oxytocin, that is produced by being kind to others is also produced by love.

In a study published in 1997, Russek and Schwartz shared the findings of 126 healthy young men in the early 1950s from Harvard who were given questionnaires about their perceptions of the love they felt from their parents.

In 1985, the authors analyzed these men for the rate of diagnosed midlife diseases (e.g., coronary artery disease, high blood pressure, duodenal ulcer, alcoholism). What they found was:

Rate of Diagnosed Midlife Diseases (heart disease, high blood pressure, duodenal ulcer, alcoholism)	
Non-loving Mom: 91%	Loving Mom: 45%
Non-loving Dad: 82%	Loving Dad: 50%
Both Parents Non-loving: 100%	Both Loving Parents: 47%
(Russek & Schwartz, 1997)	

2. https://www.huffpost.com/entry/can-kindness-cut-the-risk_b_799562 - David R. Hamilton Ph.D.

Now I'm not trying to convince you to become a replacement for an unloving parent at your place of work, but what is so interesting is that empowering others with kindness will actually create the same needed health benefits that being loved by parents can produce. Kind actions increase oxytocin in your system and the systems of those around you, resulting in decreased risk of disease.

Another side of the heart disease discussion is that, if you're not part of the solution, you are likely part of the problem. A study published by Hans Bosma, Ph.D., Richard Peter, Ph.D., Johannes Siegrist, Ph.D., and Michael Marmot FFPHM in the *American Journal of Public Health* connected the negative effects between the psychosocial hazards of work and an increase in heart disease. The study showed "the imbalance between personal efforts (competitiveness, work-related overcommitment, and hostility) and rewards (poor promotion prospects and a blocked career) was associated with 2.15 times higher risk of new coronary heart disease. Also, experiencing low job control made the odds of heart disease 2.38 times more likely. [3]

The physical health of your employees is in your hands. You can either be a contributing risk factor or you can be part of the healing process.

You must also consider the mental health of your people. Stress and injustice at work leads to a significant amount of mental health dangers and decreases organizational health.

In 2013, the National Institute of Mental Health stated that neuropsychiatric disorders are the leading cause of disability in the United

3. https://ajph.aphapublications.org/doi/abs/10.2105/AJPH.88.1.68).

States, with major depressive disorder being the most common. [4] We are becoming more aware of the alarming rate at which depression is taking a toll. According to a study conducted by Blue Cross Blue Shield, "Diagnosis of major depression has risen dramatically by 33% since 2013". [5]

Suicide is the tenth leading cause of death in the U.S., with 47,173 suicides in 2017. Of those suicides, 30,000 were the result of people suffering from depression. In addition to that staggering and heartbreaking figure, there were 1,400,000 suicide attempts. [6]

When people suffer from depression, there isn't an on-off switch they can flip when they enter the office. This isn't an "at-home" epidemic. In 2017, the Employee Assistance Professionals Association revealed that mental health (depression, grief, and behavioral conduct) is the second-leading workplace concern, following family issues. [7]

It isn't a workplace concern merely because employees are experiencing poor mental health during work hours. It's a workplace concern because if the workplace is a source of imbalance of personal efforts and rewards it directly contributes to an increased risk of poor mental health. [8]

It is also a workplace concern because depression is the leading cause of disability worldwide and is a major contributor to the overall global burden of disease according to a 2017 statement by the World Health Organization.

4. National Institute of Mental Health, "U.S. Leading Categories of Diseases/Disorders," 2013

5. https://www.nbcnews.com/health/health-news/major-depression-rise-among-everyone-new-data-shows-n873146

6. https://www.dbsalliance.org/education/depression/statistics/:: https://afsp.org/about-suicide/suicide-statistics/

7. Employee Assistance Professionals Association Survey, 2017

8. Ferrie et al., injustice at work and incidence of psychiatric morbidity: the Whitehall II study Occupational and Environmental Medicine 2006; 63: 443-450 :: https://oem.bmj.com/content/63/7/443

In *American Mania, When More Is Not Enough*, Peter Whybrow demonstrated how increased stress levels make people sick with ulcers, depression, anxiety, and high blood pressure.

As a leader, you have a responsibility to create a work environment that is beneficial to your people not detrimental. It is important for you to recognize the dangers of a toxic work environment and develop a culture that not only avoids and fights against these dangerous pitfalls but that will implement changes to create positive outcomes. You also have a responsibility as a leader to care about your company's organizational health. A toxic work environment has a significant negative impact on the bottom line and productivity of your business. In 1999, the National Institute of Mental Health Depression reported that the annual toll on U.S. businesses amounts to about $70 billion in medical expenditures, lost productivity, and other costs. The report went on to share that depression results in nearly $12 billion in losses annually due to workplace absence and another $11 billion or more in employee productivity losses due to lack of energy, decreased work habits, problems with concentration, memory, and decision-making caused by depression. [9]

The financial impact on workplaces is staggering and the suffering of workers is alarming. These are people you should care about and create a positive work environment for, yet our jobs are actually killing us.

Many employees work harder to impress bosses and coworkers than their own spouses. They sacrifice time, creativity, mental effort, and, in some cases, the only outcome for the employee is additional stress and health risk

9. The Wall Street Journal, 2001; National Institute of Mental Health, 1999

factors.

As a leader, you must stand up and say, this is not okay. You must insist on creating a work environment and culture that will not stand by while people continue to suffer. You must be someone who contributes to building people up rather than contribute to tearing them down.

The attitude of "I put up with it, and I turned out fine" is not okay.

You have a choice to make. Will your workplace be a detrimental environment to your people's physical and mental health or will you use kindness to combat the negative effects of a toxic workplace?

Creating a culture of kindness in your organization brings more joy, extends life, and improves creativity.

Luks (1998) discovered that people experienced "immediate physiological changes" as a result of volunteering and helping others:

66%	a distinct physical sensation associated with helping
50%	experienced a "high" feeling
43%	felt stronger and more energetic
28%	felt warm
22%	felt calmer and less depressed
21%	experienced greater self-worth
13%	experienced fewer aches and pains

In fact, kindness is so powerful that even just witnessing someone else be kind to another person can have a positive effect on the viewer. It reminds me of a time when I was approached in a parking lot to help someone with their dead car battery. I didn't think much of it. I just pulled my car next to hers, popped the hood, and jumped her car battery. She thanked me, and we went on our way. I went into Smoothie King to get a smoothie for my wife. When I pulled out my wallet to pay, the young man behind the counter stopped me said, "No, you're good. I saw what you did out there, helping that lady. The smoothie's on us."

Seeing me do something kind inspired him to do something kind. Inspiration to do good for others is a powerful benefit but that's not all that happens when people see others perform acts of kindness. Witnessing kindness also causes a physical reaction in our immune systems.

In a study by McClelland, McClelland, and Kirchnit (1988), students were asked to watch a film about Mother Teresa's work with the poor and sick. Those who watched the video showed a significant boost to their immune system, which lasted an hour after watching the film.

Being kind also has a special 'replacement' power. According to the Anderson (2003) model, positive emotions (kindness, other-focused love, compassion, etc.) enhance health by pushing aside the negative emotions of sadness/depression, fear/anxiety, and anger/hostility.

This is an important strategy to understand because at some point you may find yourself at a standstill with an employee who has a bad attitude. It's hard to influence an employee to change their attitude. However, you can focus on coaching and changing your employee's behavior. Positive behavior influences your employee's attitude to become positive.

I've even experienced this with my own kids. One day, driving in the family van, our three-year-old, one-year-old, wife, and I were all in foul moods. Traffic was bad, we were all tired and hungry, the baby had been fussy for a long time (she was a drive-anywhere-screamer!). In the midst of this, our three-year-old son was complaining. I tried commanding a behavior change with an emphatic, "Stop whining." It didn't work. He kept complaining. I tried reasoning. "We'll be home soon." That didn't work. He still had a bad attitude. Out of desperation and without a strategy in mind, I said, "Let's play a game." I had to quickly come up with a game on the fly. "Let's play three favorite things. We'll pick a category, and you name your three favorite things in that category." We started with movies. "What are your three favorite movies?" He listed his favorite movies and we counted them. Then, my wife and I both took a turn. We picked a new category: three favorite characters, another category: three favorite rides. Then he wanted to pick a category: three favorite animals.

Nearly instantaneously, I was able to influence a changed behavior from speaking about negative things to speaking about positive things. It was not a distraction; it was cultivating a distinct behavior change. One round into the game and his attitude had completely changed. I couldn't directly change his attitude, but I had influence over his behavior, and then a change in his behavior affected his attitude. This is an important lesson to grasp—not only for leading others but also to help influence your own attitude through behavior. The next time you find yourself with a bad attitude toward something, go for a walk, go for a drive, get out of earshot of anyone that may think you're being a weirdo, and talk out loud about positive things. Say out loud your three favorite people or, better yet, call those people and thank them for the influence they have had in your life. You will be amazed by how this positive and kind behavior changes your attitude toward your circumstances. Plus, the people you call will be affected by the kindness because it is rare to receive unsolicited, positive messages of thankfulness.

If you have an employee who has a bad attitude toward his/her coworkers redirect that behavior toward kindness. Attitude is a giant ship that is difficult to push in the direction you want it to go if you're just swimming beside it. Behavior is a small rudder. If you can influence the captain to change the behavior, you can steer that ship to smoother waters.

The Anderson model goes on to explain that there is also an increase in joy when becoming aware of others and their humanity. This emotional, physical, and psychological awakening dispels the fear and anxiety that are generated when focusing on self.

Confession time. Quite a while ago, I had to work with a difficult person. It was getting to the point that no one wanted to work with him. It felt as though I was in a complete dead end. I was only feeling frustration toward this individual.

Then, there was a moment where I was at a store, and I saw an item there I knew that individual would like. I paused and thought, "No, I don't want to get it for him because he is difficult." Then I stopped myself and, at that moment, decided to make sure my behavior was in line with what I would normally do if I really got along with someone. I love giving gifts. So, I decided to buy that item and give it to the person with this message: "I saw this and thought you'd like it." I looked for more opportunities to do kind things for this person, and it was amazing the growth that took place in the way we could communicate and the decrease in difficulty that person acted toward me. We started to get along. Kindness pushed out the frustration I had toward this individual. The kindness I showed influenced a new attitude in this individual toward me. I don't pat myself on the back for "being the bigger person." I am very thankful for the realization that changing my behavior can have a positive impact on my attitude and influence the behavior and attitude of those I'm kind to.

There are so many more positive benefits when you are kind and give your people the ability to be kind. The American Addictions Center shares on *MentalHelp.net* that altruistic individuals have better life adjustments overall and tend to see life as more meaningful. In addition, altruism is associated with better marital relationships, a decreased sense of hopelessness, less depression, increased physical health and enhanced self-esteem. Altruism also tends to neutralize negative emotions that affect the immune, endocrine and cardiovascular functions. [10]

Showing those in your circle of influence on how to go from a life of focusing on "self" to focus on others brings about a growth process. It is a bit of a paradox that the more you focus on others instead of yourself, the more you benefit and become a better version of yourself. It seems counterintuitive that in giving to others you stand to gain great benefits. Many psychologists lend a great deal of credence to the character arc of Ebenezer Scrooge in *A Christmas Carol*. The more he thinks of others and less of himself, the more Scrooge gains positivity, joy, and fulfillment. Think of how dark a tale *A Christmas Carol* would have been if the Ghost of Christmas Yet To Come was correct. Bob Cratchit without a Christmas

10. https://www.mentalhelp.net/articles/socialization-and-altruistic-acts-as-stress-relief/

dinner for his family, Tiny Tim never uttering the phrase "God bless us, everyone," and Michael Caine never singing along with Muppets to a joyful tune. We can all agree that *The Muppet Christmas Carol* is the best version of the classic story, right?

Instead of a dark outcome, the more Scrooge learns to care for others and do kind things for them, the more he dances, sings, and the happier he becomes.

"To Tiny Tim, Scrooge became a second father. He became as good a friend, as good a master, and as good a man as the good old city ever had. And it was always said of him that he knew how to keep Christmas well if any man possessed the knowledge. May that truly be said of us and all of us!" [11]

Where are you on your journey?

Are you ready to share this idea with others?

Are you already considering the strength it may take to begin this journey?

Good!

Read on...

11. source: Muppet Christmas Carol

CHAPTER FOUR
WE ONLY HEAR WHAT WE WANT TO SEE

In writing this book, I couldn't help but think about the objections people may have and questioned if I should even try to share this message.

Whenever a change is introduced, it will be met with resistance. But that doesn't mean you should give up. Bringing about a big change in the culture of a company should never be considered a passive effort. It will take a lot of passion and energy for you to implement, but the benefits will be astounding.

Merely speaking about this concept will not be enough to achieve buy-in status. You must know that going into this, the true way to fully convince people is to have them experience it for themselves. They must first see that it is something they want before they will listen and believe that it is something they need.

The reality is that not everyone will appreciate the wisdom in doing kind deeds for others:

"I don't have enough money, why would I give any away?"

"I only get one week of PTO, why would I use that for volunteering?"

"I don't want to donate gifts to strangers; I don't even spend that much on my kids."

"Someone else will do it."

"I'm too busy."

Some will turn away and refuse to hear this message because they can't see how this would improve sales or their bottom line.

Some will turn away and refuse to hear this message because they think kindness is a demonstration of weakness.

What you must accept is that you will not be able to win every person over to this new way of thinking. In the face of adversity but there are a couple truths you must hold strong to.

1. Kindness is right for your culture.

2. You must define kindness and train your people to be kind.

Many businesses and organizations have assumed their company already operates with a kind culture and assume their people already know how to be kind. It is true that everyone is capable of being kind.

But not everyone knows how to be kind. Some have been taught that taking care of their own needs is all they have time for. Some have been taught that, in order to take care of their needs, it sometimes has to happen at the expense of others. If they work for/with you…this becomes your problem. Why? Because sooner or later, a self-centered attitude will manifest itself in poor behavior toward others. You will have to mediate the offender or provide ongoing counseling for the offended. If you are the one suffering because of it, how do you handle it? If it's tolerated behavior in your organization, someone who reports the behavior often ends up looking like a complainer.

Leaders must understand that this cannot be tolerated.

It must be a clear part of your company culture, and it starts with you leading by example. Leaders must show, teach, and involve.

Show

Showing your people what you do becomes a powerful lesson when the leaders are involved. It demonstrates that it is truly a part of the company culture.

Teach

Teaching your people the why behind what you're doing is of utmost importance. Understanding the why allows people to see the lesson behind the action. It also allows them to formulate how to apply the lessons to other circumstances they encounter.

Involve

Bring them over and over. Share your enthusiasm. Allow your people to experience what it feels like to be kind to others. Give them the opportunity to build relationships with the people they work with outside of the regular work environment or a forced social outing.

Your employees' understanding of kindness needs to match what you and your organization believe.

You have an opportunity to be a leader and influencer in powerful ways.

Think about your organization. I'm sure you have a strong vision of how you want your company to grow, and you wouldn't leave that growth to chance.

You probably also have a vision of how you want your business to be run and how you want your employees feel about working for you.

Have you shared this with your team? Have you mapped out how your employees are expected to collaborate, treat each other, and respect one another or treat customers?

Let's pretend you do leave it to chance. You might be lucky to have some people on your team who try to be kind because they were taught to live that way. This was how I was for a long time. I had been taught to be kind, and I tried to be kind. But I didn't understand the impact it could have on others if I were fully intentional to teach them to be kind and give them the ability to be kind. When I was 21, I had been promoted to a management position, and I didn't understand the responsibility and opportunity that was given to me. I tried to be kind, but I wasn't a leader by any means. I had no clue how to create a culture of kindness and teach my team how to be kind. I wasn't focused on using my position to grow the people on my team. I know I did not do a good job in that role at that time.

Kindness can't be left to chance. You must proactively grow your people.

There's the old proverb:

Give a man a fish, you'll feed him for a day.

Teach a man to fish, you'll feed him for a lifetime.

That is good. That is true. When applying kindness to this proverb, in the first line you do a kind act that lasts a day or helps for one moment.

In the second line, you have taught someone to do kind things for others. Think back on your life and any selflessness that you have demonstrated to others. Can you pinpoint someone who was your example? Someone you witnessed who inspired you to make kindness a part of who you are? That's who you are to your people. When you are kind to them you become their source of inspiration to be kind to others. But it doesn't stop with just inspiring your people to be kind. Take another look:

Give a man a fish, you'll feed him for a day.

Teach a man to fish, you'll feed him for a lifetime.

Teach a crew to fish and give them a ship, fishing nets, the expectation for a boatload of fish and to teach everyone in all of the boats around them how to fish and you will feed the world.

It's not enough to teach others what kindness looks like and then expect them to follow through with being kind. It's not enough to buy someone a cup of coffee and then hope they buy the next person in line a cup of coffee because soon that chain breaks down. Please don't misunderstand: kind gestures are needed but they just are one piece of the puzzle. The other pieces that leaders can provide are the space/freedom/authority to perform kindness, along with the leading by example. Leaders must teach others how to teach others. There's a big difference in teaching subject matter vs. teaching people how to teach. If you're in a position of leadership, you have this opportunity. I've seen people who excel at this. People who teach others how to teach others. They don't just stand out as a successful individual all alone—they stand out with a full cohort of other successful people.

This is where the exponential and immeasurable potential of empowering kindness gets exciting. Because being kind to others is such an inspirational experience, it ends up spreading farther and in stronger ways than any other type of subject matter.

So, is it something you really want to leave to chance? There's so much power to unleash for good. Don't you want to craft and demonstrate the exact behavior and attitudes you want people to understand and emulate?

How much higher of a purpose and calling can you have as a leader than to empower someone to be kind?

As a leader in your company, you don't rely on assumptions for any other parts of your organization. If you want an increase in sales, you act on it. You give it more budget, more resources, thoughtful planning, and celebrate results.

How well your employees work together, perform for their leaders, and delight your customers hinges on your ability as a leader to foster kindness in your company culture.

If your employees don't see you following through with what you say, they will tune you out. You will lose credibility as a leader. I encourage you, not to act out of fear of losing credibility as a leader, but to see it as an honor to be able to influence others for good. Some people in positions of authority are confused and think the way to be a leader is to control the people under them. They unwittingly use tactics that build resentment. People who are true leaders are not controllers, they are investors. They see it as an honor and grow their people into leaders. Investors are exactly what you need more of right now because there is a lack of true leadership talent. Finding the right leaders can be challenging because perfect leaders aren't just floating around out there. Even the greatest leaders need growth in order to adopt your company culture. You must become proficient at finding people you can grow into leaders.

Hiring and firing for culture is a real and important policy; the problem is, some mishandle this. They think they can deduce in a single interview if an individual is or isn't a cultural fit. This is a misunderstanding of culture. The responsibility of culture fit doesn't solely rest upon the candidate but more heavily relies on your company to educate and empower that individual to become a culture fit.

Can someone know enough about your company to showcase during an interview that he/she knows everything about your company culture? At the most, they've only been introduced to your company through a few places, e.g., company website, social media, or perhaps a worker or two they are familiar with. Is that enough for them to really understand your culture? Anyone in an interview is going to do his/her best to show they are the right person for the job and that you should hire them.

You want to choose people who value kindness and are teachable. Let your candidates know in the interview that you have a rigorous culture training program and that you are looking for people to be fully committed to the culture of kindness. It is then up to you to make sure culture is taught and empower them to be kind leaders in your company.

There's a big difference between true culture and ambiance. Events, swag, social media presence, activities, and gifts are often misinterpreted as a culture. Culture isn't bean bag chairs and foosball tables. Culture is about the deep beliefs that make an organization truly different. Culture has the power to affect change within your people while inspiring others outside your organization. Culture can either be poisonous or positive. Empower your people to be kind and you will be amazed at the healing that takes place for your people and the health of your organization.

You have a big challenge ahead of yourself. Think back to elementary school and the dreaded group project. Why was it so dreaded? Because, inevitably, you have someone who doesn't care about others in the group and just wants to do things their way, you have another group member who only cares about the social side of group work, you have the peacemaker who tries to get the project done and is willing to give everyone equal credit, and then you have the person who just doesn't care. Well, guess what? Those kids have grown up and now they're your employees. Yes, right now you have these types of people making up your business. As their leader, you have the opportunity to teach them how you want them to work together on a team.

You provide training on software and equipment and even how to submit a PTO request. It is vital that you spend time teaching your people, how you want them to treat each other. Creating a strategy for training your people to understand the level of kindness you are expecting is an awesome opportunity to foster this movement within your company. Instead of assuming that your people already know how you want them to collaborate, or that the people you hire will read your mind and uphold your standards you must take ownership of the health of your business, and the well-being of your team. You need to fully design how you want your business to run and how you want your people to work together and then teach them extensively. Teaching them gives them the first-hand experience needed to buy-in to a culture of kindness.

Ronald Reagan said, *"The greatest leader is not necessarily the one who does the greatest things. He is the one that gets the people to do the greatest things."*

Your business can't survive with you being the greatest at each task/division in your business. If you want to scale, you must inspire others to do great things. Cultural adoption can't be assumed. You must understand how people learn. Not everyone catches on the first time they hear a message, let alone changes their behavior or character. You must be clear about your vision and culture and communicate and demonstrate it over and over. A big portion of your responsibility as a leader is to create the lens your people will make all of their decisions through. When you equip your people to use kindness as their lens to make decisions you will see improvements in all areas of your business. When you emphasize, require, implement, lead by example, hold others accountable, celebrate the wins, and promote others for their success in the efforts to empower kindness, the effort of one person, you, is implemented with everyone in your organization; they, in turn, put this effort into effect in how they interact with your customers, prospects, vendors, and third-party providers. At that point, you begin effecting change even beyond your walls. The greatest power of a culture of kindness is initiating the multiplier effect of success, improvement, and overall good things happening. Your hiring, coaching, brainstorming, teamwork, comradery, idea generation, customer service, and customer satisfaction will all improve and if fully adopted, you will have created a company that people love. Earning love from your employees and customers doesn't come from merely a great product or good service. If you want people to love your company, your company first has to love people.

Recently, I needed to hire a pest control company to handle ants during the rainy season. A friend of mine told me about a good experience he had with a pest control company, so, on his recommendation, I gave it a try. I called, they were polite, came out when scheduled, and provided excellent service. I was so pleased that I recommended the company to family and other friends. It was a win for the pest company. One referral leading to two more. They did the job proficiently. But I didn't fall in love with the company. In this competitive market with every company's reputation and reviews just one click away, it's not enough to just meet expectations. Customers are being trained all the time on what good service and great service looks like and feels like.

Let's talk about Walt Disney World. Yes, there's another chapter dedicated to Walt Disney World, and what I will cover there isn't what you think. What I cover now will be more along the lines of what you're predicting I talk about, but I assure you that, even in this little blurb, there's going to be a surprise you need to pay particular attention to.

First of all, don't tune out if you think because Disney is a multi-billion dollar company that their style of service is out of your league. Sure, they have infinite resources and can afford to conduct sweeping gestures of generosity for their guests. But what we need to see is that it is not the money that makes their gestures amazing. Their gestures are amazing because they empower all of their people to be kind.

Walt Disney World is famous for its magical moments. Some friends described a moment where their two-year-old had waited in line to meet

Daisy Duck at Animal Kingdom. Once they got to the front of the line, it was time for Daisy to take a break. Daisy spent some time with their little girl and then decided she wanted some company to walk her to her break location. She took the little girl by the hand, and together they went on a stroll through the park. After sharing that story with us, her father said, "That's why Disney is so great." To them, it was a moment made special for their daughter, but in the Disney organization, the idea of giving a little extra special moment to the guest is its targeted goal and mission. This moment that Daisy Duck gave to our friends didn't take a Disney-sized budget but it did take Disney-sized hearts. It takes your leadership cultivating a culture of kindness and empowering your people to make decisions through a lens of kindness. In an organization that isn't focused on kindness that employee may have taken their break and not taken the extra time for a guest. We wouldn't have faulted that employee for leaving and going on a break. But when you build a culture where kindness is celebrated and the power to act on kindness is afforded your people they start to do things that can mean a great deal to others.

Now, I'm not at all suggesting that the pest control guy should have tried to hold anyone's hand while performing his duties at our house. But these two examples side by side shows how much upswing there is to provide an excellent experience.

The pest control guy did his job and met positive expectations. He was trained to do his work properly and had some people skills. Daisy, though, made a guest's day magical. She was able to accomplish this because she was empowered to be kind. Freedom, autonomy, the authority to make decisions at the moment, and interaction with a guest to provide the opportunity to give extra attention to that little girl. The result, an extra-happy little girl, amazed parents, and a referral of the heart. Her parents didn't say to me, "It was a great experience. You should go." They said something greater. "That's what makes Disney the greatest." In other words, "We love it."

By empowering kindness, you unlock unlimited potential. Get your people to do a good job? That's fine; that should be expected. Empower your people to be kind, and their actions could become part of the fabric of another person's life. Their actions could bring joy and be added to someone's scrapbook and memory bank, even inspiring others to be kind.

What does Disney do to make sure its cast members are executing on the lessons learned? They hold their people accountable to be kind. Have you ever been on a call with the Walt Disney World Resort? There's a short survey, about five questions at the end of each call. One of the questions is along the lines of, "if you run a business, what is the likelihood that you would hire the cast member who just assisted you?" The answer may come naturally to you because of your experience in hiring and building teams but to the average caller, it is out of the ordinary. This hypothetical question causes the listener to make a gut decision. A gut decision that is actually based on years of fact.

A few years ago, my wife and I were house shopping. As we were standing in someone else's house with their pictures on the walls and their furniture in each room, my wife said to me, "This house feels like home." There, in an instant, with her brilliant understanding and ability to assess a lifetime of observations, she knew what home felt like. My wife and I looked at several homes we thought were nice, the right size, a good price, or location. But only one stood out—not because of the price, location, décor, or layout specifically—but because when Holly walked around that house, it felt like home to her. I trusted her judgment; we went with her gut feeling. To a lot of people that may seem peculiar. We had spent 15 minutes looking around a home that someone else had made their own. So how could it feel like home? She was not making a wild statement. For her entire life, she had been taking in places, sights, sounds, and experiences that helped formulate what she believed her ideal home to feel like. The way the mind works is fascinating. We are able to take hundreds of thousands of experiences and, in milliseconds, draw from a lifetime of stored memories to reach a conclusion. That's why a hunch from a great detective usually leads down the right track and why a mother's intuition is always right when it comes to *"having a bad feeling about this..."*

Back to the survey question. By asking a hypothetical question of hiring that Disney cast member you must rely on speculation. You didn't ask them any interview questions to determine if they should work for you. When speculation is involved, it increases the knowledge base we must access and assess from. To answer a specific question that requires no speculation, we don't have to use much judgment. We assess the immediate situation with the immediate knowledge we have.

You ask, "Can you help me make a hotel reservation?"

Boom! The cast member helps you make a hotel reservation.

You take the survey, "How was your call experience?"

You would only assess whether or not your request was met. But, add in the element of "gut instinct," and now you're assessing how well that person performed based on every other hotel customer service interaction you've ever had. How that person made you feel with just the tenor of his/her voice, whether that person's skills at building rapport lived up to your expectations of a Disney cast member. Gut instinct could even recall how in that brief moment you liked talking to that cast member because, for some unknown reason, he reminded you of your favorite uncle. Is this nonsense? Nope. It's your brain's capability to assess all those complex memories, emotions, expectations, and experiences all down to an immediate assessment with your gut. So, if it's all in your powerful mind, then how come we call it gut instinct? Or a gut reaction? The reason is our "guts" (aka digestive system) are known to carry as many as 100 million neurons, more than in your spinal cord or your nervous system. [1] Which makes our guts feel like they're actually contributing to our brain's ability to assess and evaluate situations.

This depth of understanding and assimilating your experiences is exactly what you are providing to Disney's business intelligence team. When Disney asks if you'd hiring their cast member you aren't sharing your reaction to a single scenario. It is uncovering something deeper about you. They are tapping into your heart to find out if they have actually done a good job, by using your entire lifetime of experiences as a metric.

It seems wild, but sometimes your gut is the best guide to knowing when to be kind. If you can give your people so many experiences in learning about kindness, opportunities to be kind to others and the ability to be kind to others you could help to train their 'gut instinct.' It is then

1. https://www.scientificamerican.com/article/gut-second-brain/

a lens to make decisions that come second nature to them and gives them the immediate ability to assess a situation and act appropriately in kindness.

A good example of training your gut and using gut instinct is in the interview process. Without a candidate knowing your company culture, you're having to use your gut to assess if, based on their answers, you believe they could actually do the job and become a fit in your organization. It is then up to you to train them well and teach them your company culture, so they can fully execute your vision.

Jon Gordan has said, *"Great leaders don't succeed because they are great. They succeed because they bring out the greatness in others."*

This is similar to the Ronald Reagan quote, *"The greatest leader is not necessarily the one who does the greatest things. He is the one that gets the people to do the greatest things,"* but has a slightly different focus. Reagan's quote focused on the actions that others will accomplish under great leadership. The added layer that Jon Gordan touches on is that leadership is more than inspiring others to accomplish things. There is a difference between 'great things' and 'greatness.' It is the ultimate investment in another human being when, because of your leadership, they don't just accomplish something great but they become great.

It is important for you to be a constant voice of affirmation and revelation of your team's character. It's important to convey to your people that you believe in them and trust them; then, give them the authority, autonomy, and resources to understand their greatness and perform to that standard. You will build a company full of people that don't just do great things occasionally, but the people themselves will become great and as a result, everything they do will be great. Every decision they make will be influenced by kindness.

When you empower your people to be kind, they will amaze you with their greatness.

CHAPTER FIVE

THESE ARE MY PEOPLE: THE MAGIC OF LIKE-MINDED PEOPLE SEEKING AND FINDING YOU

You will notice a tipping point and feel a momentum shift when people start to self-identify with your organization. When your company becomes known for kindness there will be people who seek out opportunities to work for you because of the desire within themselves to make a difference in others' lives and find a fulfilling purpose in their work. The momentum of what you are able to accomplish will skyrocket once people begin raising their hands to say, "I want to be a part of this," because you will begin onboarding people who already agree with your mission and will more readily adopt and adapt to the behaviors and techniques you are implementing. Rather than encountering heavy effort or friction to get the momentum going, you will be bringing on people who know-how and look for ways to add to the multiplier effect of empowering kindness. They will bring their experience and desire to be kind to your company and everyone in your organization will benefit.

The people you are attracting to come work for you may be at a number of different stages in their adoption of kindness. Once onboard, you will still need to foster their growth through the life cycle of empowering kindness.

It is important to assess their willingness to learn and grow through these stages in order to avoid opposition and friction. It's also important to determine what stage they're at in their personal growth in order to properly align them within your culture.

LIFE CYCLE OF KINDNESS IN AN INDIVIDUAL

1. Acknowledgment

The "I notice when people are kind" stage.

They must acknowledge that kindness exists. You have a responsibility to get your ideas out there so people can understand that it is a possibility.

2. Recognition of the positive

The "I should try to do more to be kind" stage.

This is the stage where the individual agrees that kindness has positive benefits.

3. Projection of self

The "I think I'll take part in that 'kind' activity" stage.

An individual who can see himself or herself in the role or desires to experience the role.

4. First experience

The "You're signing up, too? Okay, I'm in" stage.

This step brings about the need for some "rip the Band-Aid off" gumption, to break through a barrier of resistance. It's the stage where procrastination can set in hard and make a home for itself. This is a step that could require a push from someone already in your organization. What better way to get people past that first hump than to take them on a philanthropic experience during onboarding?

5. Consecutive outings to gain initial momentum

The "I've gone a few times and enjoyed it" stage.

They have to experience it multiple times in order to gain consistency with it.

6. Habit

The "I haven't missed in months" stage.

As they do this consistently for a long period of time, it becomes part of what they feel they must do. If they skip it, they have a feeling of missing it.

You may have heard that, if you do something for 21 days in a row, it will become a habit. Or perhaps you've heard that the special number is 30 days in a row. The truth is that there isn't a specific number you have to hit. I know from personal experience because I have bonded with my wife during a special, let's call it, "summer fit physique, exactly three-week solution." I've also bonded with my wife during a special, let's call it, "the complete, more than 29 but less than 31 days healthy eating plan." Do you know what happened when we encountered Day 22 with the first plan and Day 31 with the second plan? Complete and utter halt! "Finally, we're done!" It didn't turn into a habit. Why? Because even the title of the program does not suggest that you're trying to make it a habit. It gets you thinking it is a quick solution in a specific time frame; then, we have the hope it will turn into a habit because we've heard these special numbers of 21 days or 30 days until the behavior becomes a habit. Well, the truth is, you can't set the goal for the minimum number of days you think it will take to accomplish a new attitude. You have to set a goal of making it ongoing and the amount of time it will take for consecutive behavior to turn into a habit will be different for every person. For some, it could be in 21 days; for others, it could be more than two months. Have patience and keep going.

7. Identity

The "Hey, I noticed that there's a need and I wanted to help" stage.

This is the outward showing of one's self-perception. Do they consider themselves as a leader who encourages kindness? Do they pay attention to their surroundings and apply themselves to help? Do they have an internal compelling force to strive to perform in this role? They perceive themselves as someone who is kind, they actively demonstrate kindness and desire others to recognize them as someone who is kind.

8. Character

The "I can't help it. It's who I am" stage.

Kindness is truly a part of their character when it becomes who they are. When they can't help but be kind. When they base their decisions, behaviors, actions, and beliefs on their internal fortitude and trained conscience. When kindness becomes something that they can't help but follow through with (no matter how challenging), and they find their mission in empowering others to be kind. It becomes the defining factor in how others characterize them and fully expect to be treated by them. Their reputation precedes them and gives authority to their decisions and advice. They do the right thing for another person no matter how uncomfortable or self-sacrificial the effort may be.

When thinking of an example of someone who reached this stage of maturity, my mind goes to two families I went to church with growing up. One family was an older couple who had suffered the loss of a child. The other family was a young couple, and there was a day when their youngest had fallen into their pool and had not yet learned to swim. This young family was distraught. When she was thankfully revived, they were still nervous about the possible long-term effects this could have on her health. The older couple was the first in line to comfort and provide support to this young family. It was incredibly difficult for them to revisit an experience that hit so close to home, but they did it because it was part of their character to be kind. They knew what it was like to suffer such a horrible experience and resolved that they would comfort this young couple going through a similar fearful experience. What they don't realize, though, is that it has also motivated so many others, including me, as just a hearer of what they have done, to see the opportunity to use any experience as a way of connecting with others, to share in being kind and seeing how good can come from something terrible.

LIFE CYCLE OF KINDNESS IN AN INDIVIDUAL

The people you attract to join your team will all be at different stages in the kindness life cycle. They will all have different skills, talents, and abilities. If an entry-level candidate is in the early stages of the life cycle of kindness it doesn't mean you shouldn't hire them. It is your job to help them to understand and embody your company culture by empowering them to be kind, which in turn builds their character. If you are hiring someone that will have others reporting to them, it is a must that they need to be advanced in the life cycle of kindness. The character of your managers, supervisors, and leaders must be defined by kindness. They are responsible for bearing your cultural flag and keeping kindness spreading within your organization. A boss that is not kind will run people you just attracted to your company right back out the front door.

CHAPTER SIX

COMMUNICATION IS A GIFT: TREAT IT LIKE ONE

Best intentions can go awry.

To implement the culture-changing concept of empowering kindness you have to pay attention to the vehicle you deliver your message in. If you are not careful, you may preemptively bring your efforts to a halt.

To deliver a message of being kind to others, your communication must also be kind.

I love my mom. She is incredibly thoughtful and kind. But sometimes she overthinks things when it comes to picking out gifts.

I left Canada when I was 18 years old to head to university in Florida. Fact: Florida is hot, but it's even more exceptionally hot for a Canadian. Another thing to know is that my birthday is just a few days before Christmas. Well, when I went home for Christmas break, my mother bought me a birthday present. I unwrapped it and looked at the gift in bewilderment. I did not understand why she had bought me…wait for it: long-sleeved, plaid flannel button-up pajamas. The brand name on the tag was "Lounge Wear."

I was confused. I was in college, not a senior home. As politely as I could, I asked her why she decided to get me hot flannel pajamas to wear in Florida.

Her response was that she thought that I might want to wear them in the evenings around the dorm. That comment painted a picture of young men in their dorms with slippers, reading the paper before turning in for the night.

I was still confused, so I asked for further clarification.

She said that when she bought a pair of the same pajamas for my grandfather, the lady at the store said I would like to have a pair, too.

I was even more confused. I was 18 and had matching pajamas with my grandfather because of a recommendation made by a lady in the men's department at the Hudson's Bay Co.?

She then shared that I am the hardest person to shop for.

I replied in the sweetest tone: "Mom, I think I'm the easiest person to shop for, but that lady doesn't know me. You know me. You know what I would like, right?"

She answered reluctantly, "Something with Batman on it."

"Exactly."

The reason my mom was reluctant in answering that question, and why she was reluctant to get me a Batman gift is because she doesn't understand why I like Batman. She doesn't understand why I like Batman because she doesn't like Batman the way I do.

Most people are confused about gift-giving. They purchase you a gift because they like that item and want you to also enjoy it.

Because this happens often, and we want to be polite when we encounter gifts that we may not necessarily want, an expression and social expectation has been created called, "It's the thought that counts."

Well, at the risk of sounding like a meanie, I am taking the bold stance in saying this phrase is complete and utter garbage.

This is said when someone gives you a gift that you don't like. What is meant by the people who say it? They want the receiver to be mannerly and thankful to the giver in spite of the gift missing the mark, and the giver being oblivious to the fact that if they actually put some thought into it, they would know that you wouldn't like it to begin with. Here's the thing, a gift is meant to evoke joy/enjoyment from the recipient. That means the gifter needs to put thought into choosing a gift that the recipient will like. It isn't as common that a person sets his/her own preferences aside in gift-giving to think about what you would actually want and enjoy.

Why am I sharing this story?

It is an understandable experience, one that I'm sure we can all say, "Been there, exchanged that." Apply this example to the way we communicate with others. If we want to empower kindness in others, we must be thoughtful in the way we communicate.

You have to understand that everyone has different personalities just like everyone has different tastes in gifts, and the way you would be most receptive to a message is not the exact same way someone else on your team will be most receptive to a message. Deliver your message like a gift, in a way they will want to receive it. Know the people on your teams, understand their personalities and their preferred style of communication. Step outside your preferred style of communication to deliver the message to them. Put some real thought into it. If you speak to people in a way they appreciate, they will be much more receptive to your message.

There are many tests out there that are effective in helping you to understand the personality style of you and your teammates, so you can understand how to effectively communicate your vision, instructions, and requests.

Let's play out an example.

If you're a bold, get-things-done, results-driven person, you probably prefer having a brief list of top priorities that you can quickly run down and get straight to the point.

However, if you're speaking to someone who is motivated by relationships and needs assurance you care about them, they won't react well to you if you show no empathy or appreciation. First, ask how full their plate is, and connect with them on a personal level by showing you care for them, their family, and workload. If you are asking them to do something outside of their area of responsibility, acknowledge it. Let them know if you are intending for them to add the responsibility ongoing or if you just need them to cover the responsibility one time. Share with them if you are asking them to handle it because of their talent.

With each of your people, it's important to connect personally, respect their capabilities, outline your "asks," and give clear boundaries about how often you will add new responsibilities to their plates.

Clear communication is key for buy-in. You cannot get buy-in if your people quit listening because you are speaking in a way that isn't kind.

Communicating effectively in a recipient's preferred style of communication should not hide the message. You must be candid in your communication. I've heard it said by many people: "To be unclear is to be unkind." Expectations should not be shrouded in mystery. Desired outcomes cannot be left up to the imagination. Required conduct cannot be delivered through hunches, innuendo, or assumed osmosis.

You must clearly lay out SMART goals: specific, measurable, achievable, relevant, and time-oriented. This is an overly common acronym that has been around forever, but, in the exercise of everyday requests, we sometimes forget to communicate in this way. You must always hold yourself accountable to this criteria. When communicating what you hope to accomplish in your company. If you want your people to be accountable, they need to know your expectations. Your people need to know what they are getting into before they will be willing to participate.

Understand who your people are, what motivates them, and how they prefer to be communicated with. Deliver your message in an effective way that will be well received by them. Be clear on the responsibilities and goals that you want them to achieve.

Be clear when someone is missing the mark.

Be clear when someone is excelling.

Be clear when someone has transitioned from merely executing tasks to bringing fresh ideas, problems, suggested solutions, and/or passionate endeavors. Going above and beyond must not be measured by how heavily the scale tips toward work in your employees' work/life balance. It must be measured by their ability to connect with people, inspire them, create problem-solvers, and grow others to become leaders. Identify and celebrate their progress with important tangibles such as increased compensation, added flexibility in their schedule, investment in their career, and sharing their growth with key leadership, so they can be assured that their contributions are fully noted and tracked in their career path.

You must always be clear in communicating with all of your people. If you are not clear, negativity will fill in the gap. If an employee does not feel appreciated, or does not receive meaningful recognition for their contributions and growth, they will let others know about their experience. Often people think it's acceptable to keep their employees in the dark or, worse yet, hold them back out of fear that the employee will surpass them. I've seen managers repackage their team member's ideas as their own in order to gain favor with those they report to. I've seen managers give skewed reviews because they don't want their team members to get big heads or have to compensate them more than they already are. I've seen managers fail to come to an employee's defense when someone is bizarrely trying to sabotage his/her reputation or good ideas. As a leader, you have a heavy responsibility to uncover and remove these poor management behaviors and replace them with positive and kind behaviors.

You must defend your good team members when you discover people within your organization are exhibiting petty behaviors. You have the responsibility to coach your poorly behaved employees up to your standards of kindness or remove them from your organization. You also have the responsibility to lift up and celebrate those who demonstrate kindness.

In the news recently, a fourth-grade boy wore a homemade University of Tennessee t-shirt to his school spirit day. A group of kids made fun of him for his shirt. When he got back to his classroom, his teacher noticed he had put his head down and was visibly upset. She found out what was wrong and comforted him. Later, she reached out on social media to see if there would be any way UT would do something special for this boy. Well, they answered back in a big way. The University of Tennessee not only sent him some cool items, but they included hand-written notes, gifts for the rest of his class, and the exciting news that UT would put his design on a real t-shirt that could be purchased from the VolShop. They also announced that proceeds from the shirt would go to an anti-bullying campaign. The story and shirt received so much attention that the VolShop site crashed from the volume of orders. I ordered one and didn't even care I had to wait a month to get it, I was excited that the orders were doing so well! The news became even bigger as UT offered admission and a four-year scholarship to cover the boy's tuition and fees.

The message UT sent was clear. They don't stand for bullying. They want to celebrate and uplift a child who had been put down. Kindness was celebrated.

You have the opportunity in your business to eradicate behaviors that are contrary to your culture. You have the opportunity to celebrate behaviors that strengthen and build up your culture.

CHAPTER SEVEN
THE REAL REASON WE GO TO DISNEY WORLD

Maybe you're a theme park enthusiast, maybe you're not. But it is undeniable that Disney knows how to be successful in that market. What makes it stand out?

Years ago, B.C. (before children), I was a Universal Studios guy. I had an annual pass for Universal Orlando and would go to Islands of Adventure and Universal Studios frequently. Although I was a thrill ride junkie I still saw a key differentiator Walt Disney World brought to the table. I remember speaking with friends about theme parks and saying, "Universal has the rides and design for me (superheroes…I mean, c'mon!), but Disney is an incredible example of customer service." I saw Disney cast members as more attentive, keeping the parks cleaner, having a better reputation for customer service. There are books like *The Disney Way*, which I read and loved. I had such a positive impression of Disney World.

It wasn't until A.D. (after dad-ing) that my impression of Disney turned into an experience with Disney. When my son was one, we bought annual passes to Walt Disney World. It was then that we were lucky enough to experience some "pixie dust."

What is "pixie dust?" Well, besides being the special ingredient that makes the characters in Peter Pan fly, it is also the term Disney enthusiasts use to describe actions by Disney cast members to make the experience magical for guests.

There was the day my wife and I were selected on our anniversary to sit in a VIP section to watch the parade. Another day, we were pretty much the only guests swimming in the pool at a Disney hotel, and a couple of cast members came over to ask my son if he was having fun, and unprompted he made up a story: "Remember that one time when we saw a hippo named Gloria?" They laughed and acted interested, and then less than an hour later showed up at our hotel room with balloons and a plush hippo wearing a Disney name tag that read "Gloria" for him and a baby Minnie Mouse for his five-month-old sister. On another trip, we were celebrating our wedding anniversary, and, to spark some magic memories of our Hawaiian honeymoon, I surprised my wife by taking her to the Luau at the Polynesian Resort. Truth be told, we definitely could not afford to stay at the Polynesian Resort, so we were staying at one of the Value Resorts. Unfortunately, our room wasn't ready when we arrived, and as a result, we had no place to get changed for our dinner. The front desk cast member asked me to wait a moment. She went into the back office then returned to share with me that they didn't have a room for us at the Value Resort. Instead, we'd been upgraded to the Polynesian Resort at no extra cost. Plus, she took me into the gift shop to pick out a special gift for us to commemorate our celebration.

With these things happening for us and our kids, we have become Disney loyalists. We can't consider letting our passes expire because we know we may not be able to handle the withdrawals.

What is so special isn't just the magical experiences and the hope of getting free stuff. Sure, those magical moments are enjoyable; they make for great stories, and it builds Disney's word-of-mouth referrals.

But what I love even more about Disney, what I really, really, REALLY love about Disney, is that, guaranteed, no matter who I talk to there, kindness is part of their character (not the costume kind, but the inner character). They will be kind and say hello. They will have a conversation. This common courtesy of being kind to everyone is missing in a lot of everyday circumstances.

So how does Disney get it right?

They empower their cast members to be kind. Their cast members are given the ability to make a guest's day magical. Its brand is kindness, but they use a word that's a little more from a fairy tale, "Magic."

I love seeing our kids' faces light up when they are at Disney. It's special, but not nearly as magical as the moment our six-year-old boy tied in a game of musical chairs and said, "It's okay, he was here first," demonstrating his love for the game and the people he is playing with more than anything else. When I praised him for it, I could see the true joy within him. It radiated so much stronger than anytime he had a great day at Disney.

Why do we love going to Disney? Why do we put up with the long lines, walking on the face of the sun? (aka Orlando in summer) If the heat and exhaustion don't cause us to faint, then the prices will. But we keep coming back. Why? Because kindness is king.

Kindness melts away so many objections. We will pay more, drive farther, and deal with more inconveniences to do business with, or work for people who are kind.

A few weeks ago, we were getting quotes from contractors to renovate our back patio to remedy frequent flooding. One of the contractors showed a superior product, competitive pricing and a favorable timeline to complete the project. I thanked him and let him know I had one more appointment, then I would compare and decide. At that point, he became aggressive and made bold and derogatory claims about the other contractors I had been meeting with, even though he didn't know who they were. At that moment, the only thing I could think of was that I didn't want to spend any more time around that type of communication.

Whereas, with Disney, it's comforting to know that my kids can trade pins with any cast member, and it will be a positive interaction. Every transaction and experience is met with kindness.

When your company can achieve that "next level" reputation and culture, it begins to attract people who want to exhibit kindness in every area of their life.

You get people who desire to work for you because they find joy in the culture—not necessarily the tasks they must perform. I mean it's still as hot as lava in Orlando, but they want to put smiles on people's faces. They want to be kind, and they are looking for a place where they can have the freedom to do it. When you begin attracting people who want to make kindness a part of their daily lives, you have unlocked something special and those people will bring about some true magic.

It goes beyond dependable, polite customer service, being surprised with a free Mickey ice cream bar or a hotel upgrade.

In January of 2018, a guest named Robert Leibowitze was seen walking around the Magic Kingdom wearing a t-shirt that said, "In need of a kidney. O-Positive," and his phone number. Guests and strangers took some pictures of the shirt and posted it on social media. The post was shared 32,000 times that day and 90,000 times by the end of the week. Their desire to show kindness led people to make a difference. For Robert, the difference was life-altering. Four people flew to New York and a match was found.

When the donor, Richie Sully, reached out to Robert, he left a voicemail saying, "Hi, my name is Richie. I saw your post, and I'm O positive. I have an extra kidney, and you are more than welcome to it."

A cast member named Steven Crow saw the story on social media and thought, "Wow! Isn't that cool? It would be cool to be able to do something like that." Two months later, the exact same opportunity presented itself for Steven. Whether it was divine intervention or a complete coincidence, a man by the name of Adam Hedrick came to Disney World on vacation wearing a t-shirt his daughter had made for him that said, "I need a kidney O-positive" with his phone number. Adam happened to order a meal on this trip at Steven's register. Steven saw the shirt, and, knowing he had a matching blood type, he wrote down the phone number. In speaking with Steven, he shared with me his internal thought was only, "Because I can do this good thing, I should."

Steven got the ball rolling to donate a kidney to a stranger in the same fashion he had been inspired by a few months earlier.

Steven shared that he didn't realize what a huge impact this was going to have on Adam and his family. He didn't think much about how he would be saving a life, saving a wife from becoming a widow, saving children from losing their father. It wasn't until they were in the hospital room before the surgery that Steven spoke with Adam's wife, Shawna. Hearing her express her gratitude, Steven began to realize what a long-lasting impact this would have on the family he was helping. It was a moving experience not only for the Hedrick family but also for Steven.

Steven also didn't realize is the ongoing impact this story will have on people, inspiring them to be kind just as he was inspired by seeing someone else's kindness. An incredible side effect of his actions that wasn't covered by the news was how his example gave those around him the inspiration to be more attentive to others and be more intentional about being kind.

Disney has also had a similar effect of inspiration on many of their guests. Guests who want in on the fun of being kind to others and make their day magical. I remember overhearing a mother and father speaking to their son while we were waiting to board the Magic Kingdom train, "Okay, now we just have to find a boy who is having a birthday today." I thought they were playing some kind of theme park bingo game, and, by coincidence, it was our son's birthday. I turned to them and said, "It's our son's birthday." With big smiles on their faces, they said, "Oh good, here you go. Happy Birthday." And they handed our son a Disney pirate flashlight. We rode the train, and I asked them about what they were doing. They said that they get to come to the parks often, and, instead of buying gifts for their kids, they like to have their kids give gifts to other kids. How cool is that?

Disney has done an incredible job of empowering kindness in its cast members and has earned such a reputation that they are able to attract people who want to be free to be kind to others in their occupation.

They have built a reputation as a company that cares about others, a company that is aware of their guest's experiences and genuinely cares about making them memorable and positive.

Disney isn't the only company that can enjoy the mission and benefits of a culture of kindness. You also have the opportunity to create an environment that empowers kindness, attracts those who are kind and, as a result, creates a multiplier effect of kindness, inspiring others to try it for themselves and discover just how good it feels to be kind.

Who wouldn't want to be in a place surrounded by people who are always on the lookout for ways to be kind and to teach others how to be kind?

Who wouldn't want to participate and contribute to that ongoing message?

I go to Disney because I want to be surrounded by people who go out of their way to be kind and make a day magical. Because, honestly, I would love to experience kindness every day.

This is exactly why I live with the mission to empower kindness and desire to inspire you to do the same. I want those kind moments in the place I work. I want those kind moments in the places I do business. I want those kind moments in my family life. I want those kind moments in my neighborhood. I want to see those kind moments when I turn on the news.

I want those kind moments in the lives of the people I worship with. I want those kind moments stamping out negativity all over. And I want those kind moments for you in your life and the lives of those you love and have an opportunity to influence.

Now that I'm thinking about it, I'm longing for more of those moments right now... I need to renew our Disney passes.

CHAPTER EIGHT
EMPOWERING KINDNESS AT WORK

It is my dream that leaders of organizations would see the value of empowering their people to be kind. I believe that being kind to others and giving your people the ability to be kind leads to a more fulfilled work experience and overall better life. I don't believe there's a distinction between work and life. We each have just one life on this Earth, and it's too short to waste any of it not being kind.

To your people, you must become the CEO of empowering kindness:

Chief Empowerment Officer

What does it look like?

This culture shift needs to be fully supported by you and your leadership teams if you want it to be effective. You must lead by example first by implementing priority changes within your organization.

There are a few buckets that you should be focusing on as you build out a culture for your people.

TIME. TALENT. TREASURE. TRUST.

Time

Free up your people's time. Give them extra time off to do philanthropic altruistic good deeds. Give them time in their day to be kind to each other.

Talent

Free up your people's talent. Reward them for applying their abilities in areas that help others.

Treasure

Free up your people's treasure. Compensate them fairly, so they have the flexibility to do kind things with their finances—or let them use allocated charitable funds from your company to do good for others. Consider giving them an annual philanthropy bucket that they can spend on a charity or organization of their choice.

Trust

Trust your people. Give them the autonomy and authority to make decisions that feel right to them. Give them the flexibility to pursue and introduce solutions that may seem outside their scope of work. They are closest to your customers and know what they need to reward or take care of customers. This may look different for each business based on size and focus, but there are always ways to exhibit trust in your people.

I recall a story someone shared with me about a customer calling into a support desk. The customer had accidentally paid for two subscriptions on one account to a famous dating site. The agent wanted to take care of the customer and make it right. The agent decided the way she would make it right would be to refund both subscriptions. I thought, Wow! What a great move by the agent. I was hoping the story was going to end with the customer becoming a raving fan and the leadership in the organization celebrating the agent who took the poor experience of a customer and made it right.

Instead, the story continued with the manager reprimanding her for refunding both accounts.

I was disappointed by the conclusion of the story. It was being shared with a group of customer service managers. I was just a guest, but I wanted to shout out, "Wait a minute!" This speaker was instructing all of these managers that the kind agent was wrong, and the proper action would have been to reprimand this agent. I was confused. This company has a heart in its logo! Why would she want to teach these managers that kindness is wrong? If any business should represent love and kindness, it is a company with a heart in its logo. The agent showed kindness to a customer. What if, instead of reprimanding her, they said, "Great work. Let's talk to that customer and see how much they appreciated the service." Then, call that customer, ask if they had a great experience, and what the likelihood would be of them remaining a loyal customer when it's time to renew their subscription? Even better: "Would you mind leaving a review or recommending us to some friends?" More than likely that agent's actions would have converted her into a lifetime customer (or at least until she finds true love). Not to mention all the referrals to her other single friends.

We can't be perfect, but we can be great at fixing the mistakes that are made. It's in those moments when you actually get to win the battle of creating a great experience for your customer and a tremendous feeling of empowerment for your employee.

When will you see results?

You could be wondering when you will begin to see results in your people.

Let's begin with a warning: the truth is there's no shortcut to making this a reality. You won't see pure true results in your people if you do this for the wrong reasons. Hiring a PR firm to take pictures of you with disadvantaged children won't achieve the positive benefits that sincerely performing acts of kindness will create. Another truth is that this shouldn't be looked at as though it's a destination. Empowering kindness is an ongoing journey. It is a dedication to a belief—not to a goal for the quarter or a new policy document. Change takes time. It moves slow, and you mustn't give up.

Although it will be slow to create a full culture of empowering kindness, it is true that people may experience a level of satisfaction their very first time doing kind things for another person. But the true strength comes from the ongoing growth in the individual and the beneficiary of the kindness.

Choose a group/charity to connect with and give, give, give. It's difficult to make an effective impact with only one act.

If you maintain an effort and focus your resources on a continued partnership, what may seem like a small influence at first will eventually accumulate into a large impact over time. Having a direct connection with those in need is exactly the type of group activity to incorporate into your company schedule.

Giving your people the opportunity to connect with the recipients of their kindness allows your people to understand how impactful dedicating yourself to someone else can be.

A church I'm familiar with had several members who decided to help a women's shelter during the holidays. They asked if there was a need for gifts. The church members were able to fulfill a whole bunch, if not all, of the requests for gifts for ladies and their kids.

That was good.

They gave some fish.

Soon, they found out there was a need for certain classes on cooking, personal finance, résumé building, and many other skills and hobbies. The organizers started to see a difference in the lives of the ladies and kids because they were learning.

They taught to fish.

With trust built, the organization saw improvements in the lives of the ladies and healing taking place. From there, the organization invited them to teach parenting classes. Being a church, they let the organization know that the parenting lessons they would share would have a biblical foundation. The organization agreed. Again, they were well received and provided growth and empowerment to these ladies. The influence was so helpful that, when many of the ladies completed their program, they started attending worship services and becoming a part of that church.

They fished together and they felt loved.

Think back to the first interaction between the two groups. If the church members had only given toys and gifts, it would have been nice and helpful, but gifts wouldn't have been enough to build relationships or investment in the women and children at the shelter. The commitment and ongoing dedication between the groups got them to the point of love and connection. As a result, they impacted many lives. This is the maturing of empowering kindness. It's not just about doing something nice for someone once and moving on. It's all about helping others grow and become empowered to be kind.

That's a church, but what's a business to do? You may have a school close by that could benefit from a once-a-year donation, but it would be even more helpful to partner with that school and send your people as volunteers for tutoring or donating money to each teacher to help them with school supplies or costs. One-time donations are helpful to schools, but if you truly focus empowering kindness, investing your people as ongoing assistance could possibly reshape the lives of those kids at that school.

How do you get there? What do you have to do within your organization to get your people to the point of empowering kindness?

Let's talk about some practical scenarios and everyday situations that you can focus on to empower kindness in your workplace.

1. Care for Your Company's Reputation

Start when a person first begins with your company. Is it on their first day of work? Nope, it's when they are first introduced to your company or organization. What have they heard about your company? Does your company have a positive reputation in the community? Do your current employees speak highly of their experience working at your company? Your current employees need to be part of your mission; they need to see it, believe it, and experience it to speak about it in a positive way. Do you have an online presence where people can be introduced to your company culture of empowering kindness?

Having a mature culture that is well-known in your community isn't as simple as answering these few questions. It is something you must keep a pulse on. It is important to evaluate the progress you make in adopting kindness as part of your culture. Monitor the growth of your new hires as they make their way through your new efforts. Evaluate their job satisfaction. Track how your people are speaking about your company as they move on to new adventures.

2. Be Clear in Your Job Postings

You need to get this right. If you want to attract the right person to join your company, you need to provide the right information. Anyone who joins your company or team must have an incredible interest in being kind.

3. Prepare for Interviewing Your Candidates

Ask for specific examples of times they have helped others. Call their references and ask about times when people who reported to them were promoted and how the candidate contributed to elevating their employees. You can even go as far as setting up an opportunity for them to be kind to a stranger in your lobby or elevator. Have someone posing as an applicant spill their résumés on the floor and share how nervous they are. See how your actual applicant reacts. Share within the interview what was observed and what you expect moving forward.

4. Invest in Your Onboarding Process

Onboarding should not be merely filling out a direct deposit slip and making insurance selections. Your onboarding should be treated as an opportunity to introduce your new hires to the culture and expectations you have as an organization.

Your onboarding should be at least two to three days of making employees feel welcome and a valuable part of the team.

You are trying to show them you care about them, and a perfect way to show someone they are welcome is to show them that you have prepared ahead of time for that person's arrival and that you have wonderful things to teach and share.

Here are a few ideas you may want to include as you build out a proper onboarding plan.

- Have a rep from each department or team speak for 15–20 minutes to introduce them to the team and what they do.
- Have an internal culture evangelist present on the fundamental principles of the company culture. (More on this in Ongoing Culture Evangelism.)
- Prepare a space for them with a welcome kit on their desks. It

should include everything they need to do their job: computer, monitor, mouse, chair, wastebasket, notepad, pen, branded shirt/drinking bottle, favorite snacks, and company-branded tchotchkes, Post-its, tissues, an Amazon gift card for desk decor, fan, lamp, hand-signed note, welcome banner. If you're on a big campus, be sure to give them a map of the facility with photos of key role players and do a site tour or an introduction/scavenger hunt.

- Be sure their technology is set up and ready to use. Assemble their machine, load all their programs, have their username/email/phone set up, have step-by-step directions for accessing their accounts.

- Plan a social introduction. Bring in breakfast or lunch and propose a toast to welcome your new team members. Place a jar of candy on their desks to entice people to come over and say hello.

- Be prepared to answer their questions. Assign people who love to assist and answer questions. Have a new hire user forum where people can *upvote* topics and award people who ask questions and give answers.

5. Invest in Ongoing Culture Evangelism

Give employees the knowledge/preparation to feel confident in the position you are asking them to fulfill. Provide a chain for getting their questions answered and demonstrate the expectations. Be clear when people are performing to the expectations and when they're missing expectations.

In addition to skill/process/tool training, there must be culture and thought leadership training. You can't assume that your employees know what you're thinking or how you want your business to be run. Talk to them about your higher values. Show them the vision of the company. This doesn't mean you're sharing sensitive information, but it does mean that you must clearly communicate and celebrate the values of your company. Don't just say, "Read a book." Develop a thought leadership training program with a culture evangelist role. This was a program I began at a large company. The CEO would often reference quite a few thought leadership books and say that the company's culture was based on these books. They were books that I absolutely loved and believed in. I even had the great privilege of meeting the authors and directing their keynote presentations when they were guest speakers at the company's conferences. I wanted to capture the personal experiences I was able to feel and share it with the new colleagues. I know I'm nowhere nearly as talented and brilliant as those authors, but it did give new hires a personal introduction to important messages of culture. You can find someone in your organization who can fill this role. There are people who walk among you who are already highly passionate about your company culture. Ask. I'm sure they would love to and be honored to be the culture evangelist. Expose each employee to these lessons in onboarding and bring them back every month.

6. Lead by Example

This is where many people think they can farm out the work. Some feel they are above their own company culture. They feel as though these behaviors are good for others, but they have more important things to do.

You must be completely honest with yourself. Does your leadership team buy-in to your company culture and lead by example?

Do not live in denial. Do not say you are something you are not. If your organization's core values are not true or your leadership is not upholding what your organization claims to be the culture, you must begin making changes to realign how you feel, act, value others.

If you have a leadership team that believes they don't have to lead by example, it will cause a ripple effect of dissension against what you claim to be your company's core values. The people one layer below your leaders will follow in their steps and begin to reject the core values as well.

Your culture change has to happen from the top down and involves time, talent, treasure, and trust.

7. Compensate and Appreciate Your People

Entrepreneurs, you've dedicated much of your time, talent, and treasure to get your idea into a real working and thriving business, and not too many people are going to be as passionate as you are about your idea. That's okay. People are allowed to have different motivators than you. People are allowed to have their family as their top priority. Part of that lifestyle may be to spend as much time with their family as possible. Don't bother that employee during family time. Be organized enough that you don't have to take over someone's life outside the eight hours you've agreed are part of their schedule.

Pay fairly... this is a job, not a volunteer position. Fair market value; don't ask for discounts.

8. Care for the Employee

Be truthful and connected to your culture. Know your people and know their feelings toward the culture. If you claim your company believes in a work-life balance culture, then uphold it. If you claim you have unlimited PTO, don't guilt-trip your people for taking time off. Make your people leave and go home. Shut off the lights at 5 p.m. Don't send emails on the weekend or at night. Don't contact your employees when they're on vacation. When you do, you're setting an example that this is the behavior you expect. Send flowers when they're sick and don't include a note asking when they're returning to work. Care about them. Have private, frank conversations to support them when they're going through challenging times. You're in a unique position, where people are counting on you for their livelihood in exchange for their time and contribution. Don't forget that your company is not successful without them. No leader has ever said, "Call the best software we have into the room so we can solve this dilemma." It is your people who come to your aid with ideas and solutions. Your people don't negotiate with you every time they create a piece of work or contribute an idea to your company. You, in turn, should not negotiate with them every time they need to come in late because their kid is sick or need some extra PTO when a close family member has passed away. You need them more than they need you, and, when you treat them well and care for them, they, in turn, will care for you in amazing ways.

9. Celebrate Different Opinions

Steve Jobs said, "It doesn't make sense to hire smart people and tell them what to do; we hire smart people so they can tell us what to do."

It's important to share with employees what is scientifically correct to do and what is an artistic preference. For over six years I was in charge of video production for an over $1 billion software company. Over those six years I directed hundreds of videos. There are some things: sound quality, video quality, lens focus… that aren't open for opinion. They have to be done the right way. However, there are many things that are open to opinion. A good leader when dealing with matters of artistic preference, will be sure to let employees know when there is room to contribute. Empower people to be creative in their problem-solving and expression of ideas. Let them describe their work. Let them explain what they were hoping to accomplish. Ask them if there's anything they would want to change in their project or if they are satisfied and proud of their work. Then, step away and let them make their own improvements.

If you do need to offer feedback, it's important to let them know the difference between feedback and mandated change. In other words, feedback is giving your impression, what stood out to you, and what you understood the message to be, whereas mandated change may be specific about restrictions for the project such as, "We only have two minutes for the video, and you submitted it at 2:30. I need you to cut it down." Your goal in giving feedback and mandated change should not be to get everyone to copy-and-paste your artistry or train them to make the exact same brushstrokes as you. Your goal should be to provide your people with space, canvas, and opportunity to exercise their creativity. As a leader, your job is not to try to make carbon copies of yourself but to give lanes to your people and remove obstacles, so they can exceed what you were able to previously accomplish on your own.

If you do not provide this space for autonomous thinking and creativity, a challenge you will face is people uniting over exclusion rather than inclusion. They will confuse the pursuit of true culture for seeking a homogeneous people who think exactly alike. They will unite in excluding anyone who thinks differently than them. For growth, though, you need people who share different opinions, perspectives, and, at times, even oppose your ideas. What has to be agreed upon, though, are the rules of engagement. There's no room for someone who is mean even if they have great ideas. There's also no productivity if everyone gets along and regurgitates the ideas of the highest-ranking official in the room.

10. Allow for Mistakes

If you throw the book at people whenever they make mistakes, they will become risk-averse and never try. They will just repeat what you have already said and try to guess what it is you're thinking and what you want them to do or say. If you celebrate mistakes and give people the opportunity to go big without fear of failure, you will build people who bring new ideas to the table instead of a heaping helping of mundane ideas. The types of mistakes you should never accept, though, are how people are treated. If someone mistreats another person, it must be addressed immediately. It should not be tolerated.

Someone who is allowed to mistreat others without reprimand for their behavior will become a monster. Allowing that person to rise in power will result in a lot of people being pushed aside and treated as commodities instead of the contributing people they are.

11. Foster Kind Brainstorming

Establish respect during green-light brainstorming. This may sound over the top, but the way people listen and respect each other in these sessions should be as though they believe that the next idea they hear could be the best idea they've ever heard in their life.

Get every idea on the board, look for crossover, group ideas together, make links between ideas. Ideas that seem in opposition to each other may just be building blocks for each other. Find recurring themes across all of them and bubble the most powerful solutions to the top.

Once you have begun sourcing your people for ideas and assimilating these ideas into a plan, there will be some parts that you have to say no to or leave behind. It's important to be careful to be thankful for each person's idea and kind to the individual who has shared his/her ideas. Don't use it as a judgment ground or a way to keep score.

You must build a culture that has a clearly defined expectation of rules of engagement but room for differing opinions on content and strategies. There must be a clear cut-off of the idea/brainstorming stage, then enter into an all-hands-on-deck phase. Once the decision is made, everyone needs to get behind it. No saboteurs. After an agreed-upon amount of time and evaluation, adjustments can be made and retried.

THE KEY STAGES OF KIND BRAINSTORMING

Brainstorming
all ideas welcome, no personal attacks

Decision
vote/commit

Promote
move forward

Evaluate
determine what is working and what is not working

Adjust
pivot and retry

12. Be an Expert at Coaching

One of the main focuses of empowering kindness is helping people to grow beyond their position. If there is ever any concern about the performance of someone who reports to you, it must be addressed with specific feedback on the performance and a clear understanding of what would have been preferred. Give your employees an opportunity to take the instructions and live up to the expectations you have provided. Most people want to do a good job. If there are no specific details about their lack of performance or how they can make it better, there is no value in bringing it up.

Coaching isn't just about addressing what is wrong with what an employee is doing. There must be ample focus on the wins and growth that an employee demonstrates. Celebrating their achievements and encouraging their efforts must be a significant part of your coaching plan.

When empowering kindness becomes your defining culture, you will be amazed at the rate at which you unlock the potential within your organization.

Humans are anthropologically designed to thrive and perform at their mental and healthful peak when they are being kind to others. You feel safe, welcome, wanted, and know that you are free to contribute your ideas without fear of a bad one ruining everything for you. People open up and share ideas if they know the people around them are supportive, listeners, trustworthy, and truly want to win together.

I don't suppose you can relate to an experience I had. I shared a new idea that was a bit risky but could have great upswing. I was shot down by the person I reported to and was told the idea was dumb. The next day in another meeting with higher-ranking executives, that person shared their ideas, and no one was getting on board with any of them. They quickly ran out of their own ideas and decided to share my idea as their own. The higher-ranking executives loved it, yet no credit or reward was given to me. This happens to people in businesses every day, and many of us want better.

We want to work for people who are honest, who care about us and provide a safe environment for us to share our ideas and receive credit for them. We want leaders who build us up. We want coworkers we trust, who we can care about and know that they care about us. We want the place we spend the majority of our time and lives to be a welcoming environment that we enjoy being a part of.

The only way we get there is by empowering kindness.

CHAPTER NINE
EMPOWERING KINDNESS EVERY DAY

Here we are in the final chapter of this book. I hope that the message here resonates with you and that you will aspire to be the leader who empowers kindness in your circle of influence. Some of the principles and concepts in this book were described in a way to make it practical to implement in an office or working environment, but that shouldn't be the only place we apply the practices of empowering kindness.

I encourage you to take the message to heart and be thoughtful to look for opportunities in all aspects of your life and circles of influence to make it a part of your character.

Here's a framework to understand how empowering kindness can be applied in any circumstance in your everyday life and the circles of influence you are blessed to have.

In order to be effective, look at situations and people with an entrepreneurial spirit.

1. Be observant for needs/problems

Look up. Get off your cell phone. Devote time. If you're not involved with other people, the likelihood of them sharing their needs/problems with you is low.

As you begin to observe your surroundings and discover any needs or problems, get feedback from others to try to understand if you're in touch with the situation. See if others are noticing the same needs or problems you've been observing. Make sure you are not approaching it with an attitude of complaining. There's a big difference between asking if someone has also noticed there's a problem and wanting to help versus only complaining about problems.

Early in this stage when you are exploring to see if others are noticing an issue, you may encounter people who want to offer an early and sometimes dismissive conclusion. They may say something like, "Yes I've noticed. But that's their problem." This reaction bothers me. Not everyone is equipped to pull themselves up by their bootstraps and create their own solutions. They may be suffering from this problem; I often follow-up with the question, "Has anyone tried to help them?" Typically, the answer to that is, "No" or "I don't know." When someone is dealing with a problem and having a difficult time getting themselves out of it, that doesn't necessarily mean they want to remain in that situation. Some people are not able in every situation to recognize the path to overcoming their problems. So, if you are able, why shouldn't you be looking to help them?

2. Build a plan

After you clearly understand the problem/need, it's important to give thoughtful consideration to establishing a plan.

I love the quote that's associated with Henry Ford: "If I asked people what they wanted, they would have said 'faster horses.'" I know a lot of people share that he didn't say this, but I still believe in the truth of the statement. There's room for feedback but at some point; there also needs to be the introduction of a solution that hasn't been tried before to achieve results that haven't been reached before. Get creative. Tackle the problem effectively. Ask yourself, "in an ideal world, how would I like to see this plan executed?"

Consider the resources and time that will be needed. Take your end date and work backward to the current day marking milestones. Make a list of people that you would like to assist you. Get approval/support from anyone you may need permission from and/or buy-in from your team. Once you have a thumbs up on the plan, get to work!

3. Execute the plan

This is the "getting over the first hump" step where many people get stuck. There's a lot of excitement in coming up with a solution in a brainstorming session, but it's a lot harder to actually get the gears in motion. That's why it's so important to remind ourselves about this step. You may have heard the analogy of the difference between a thermometer or a thermostat: a thermometer is someone who can say, "It's too cold" or "it's too hot" but can't do anything about it. However, a thermostat can say, "It's too cold," then kick the furnace on to warm the place up. Make the commitment to not only notice a need for change but actually act upon it.

4. Inspire and invite others to join you

This is a vital step that could get skipped by a lot of people who are type-a or lion personalities. You may want to do everything yourself and you may have reasons:

"It's just faster if I do it."

"I know what I want, so it's easier if I do it."

"I don't want to give up control."

Whatever your reasons, if you truly want to empower kindness, inviting others and getting their assistance and buy-in will generate success for even more people. Everyone learns and benefits more when they are involved in the work rather than just observing.

5. Teach them steps 1–5

You can't be the only person with ideas. You must teach others how to problem solve. Share with others your secret recipe. Show them how you accomplished what you did. Remove the mystery and show them how they can see a problem, create a plan, execute on the plan, invite and inspire others to join and then how they, too, can teach others these steps in the process. If you pass this along, you give people the power to bring about an immeasurable amount of good in their lives and the lives of others.

EMPOWERING KINDNESS IS HARD

Remember that changing behavior/mindset can take a lot of time and effort. Imagine pushing a giant boulder up a hill. You have to put all of your efforts into it. If you take your hand off the boulder or let up for one second, it will roll backward. Or, when you do make progress, you may not even realize the progress you're making. Your perspective is limited because you are busy doing the work, feeling every drop of sweat. It's much easier to see your progress when you finally take a step back to admire how far you've come. When investing in others, it is difficult to see your progress because the differences you are making in their lives happen on the inside. Not too many people thank those who have taken the time to lead and invest in them. It may not be that we want attention or adoration, but when you're working hard at something and seeing very little results, it is helpful to receive feedback that you're at least going in the right direction. If the feedback doesn't come right away, it may be that, down the road, someone you influenced or inspired may turn back and let you know about the impact you have made on them.

For a handful of years after college, I taught theater at a performing arts school. I really didn't know if I was making any sort of positive impact. I was just focused on getting the work done and staying busy. Flash-forward several years and a post showed up on Facebook from a mother of one of my former students. She said, "She's graduating high school next week! And her interest is in film and she says thanks to you!"

On the night of her graduation, she added to the post, "Literally just walked across the stage and accepted an art scholarship from Plant City Art Council!"

I was thankful to receive that feedback for a couple of reasons. First, because I hadn't thought I was making much of a difference. Second, it made me realize how few times we may ever receive positive feedback that we are on the right path. It is easy to get caught up in the day-to-day and view our challenges one inch in front of our faces, blocking us from seeing that we have moved our gigantic boulder another inch. Or that we, finally, in our efforts, have inspired someone else to get their boulder rolling. It is important to see that our influence is strong enough to inspire someone to choose the direction of his/her life. In your efforts to empower kindness, you will have an influence for the better in people's lives. They may not always share with you what it means to them. It could be because they assume you already know.

Whether or not you get feedback, don't stop. Whether radio silence or adoption at a snail's pace, keep down the path of empowering kindness no matter the adversity you face. As long as your clock is running, you are still composing your symphony. It's a symphony that may be played in other's lives that you may never know about. Bruce Springsteen doesn't know the countless rebellious teenagers who have pounded out *Born To Run* in their parent's garage. But just because he hasn't heard back from every kid who ever belted out the lyrics, "I wanna know if love is wild Babe, I wanna know if love is real," doesn't mean the boss should ever stop rocking.

The goal of this book is to uncover the real facts behind a life filled with joy and to uncover the power already within you to inspire and impact the lives of others.

I sought out these answers because, long ago, a couple of Bible verses were written that promised a better life if we are kind to others. I believe these verses because of my faith, but I also wanted to go on a fact-finding mission. In Ephesians 6:10, it says, "For we are His workmanship, created in Christ Jesus for good works, which God prepared beforehand so that we would walk in them." I believe this is a powerful summation of the purpose of our lives, and it makes sense that, if God created us and created good works for us to perform, we would stand to benefit from them.

Another verse that rings in my ears on this topic is in Galatians 6:9: "Let us not lose heart in doing good, for in due time we will reap if we do not grow weary."

Being kind isn't guaranteed to be the easy way, but it is the way we were meant to be. Please join me in this. Be kind, teach others to be kind, give your people the ability to be kind, and enjoy seeing the good you're doing make a difference in the lives of others.

Made in the USA
Columbia, SC
25 March 2020

89868639R00068